LA FEMME

LA FEMME PETA

DAWN CONNOLLY

ECW PRESS

CANADIAN CATALOGUING IN PUBLICATION DATA

Connolly, Dawn
La femme Peta: the unauthorized biography of Peta Wilson

ISBN 1-55022-385-2

1. Wilson, Peta, 1970– . 2. La Femme Nikita (Television program). 3. Television actors
and actresses – Australia – Biography. I. Title.

PN3018.W54C66 1999   791.45'028'092   C99-931996-5

Cover and text design by Tania Craan
Photo imaging by Michael Arismandez
Layout by Mary Bowness
Printed by Transcontinental, Beauceville, Québec

Distributed in Canada by General Distribution Services,
325 Humber Blvd., Etobicoke, Ontario M9W 7C3

Distributed in the United States by LPC Group-Inbook
1436 West Randolph Street, Chicago, Illinois, USA 60607

Published by ECW PRESS
2120 Queen Street East, Suite 200,
Toronto, Ontario, M4E 1E2
www.ecw.ca/press

The publication of *La Femme Peta* has been generously
supported by The Canada Council, the Ontario Arts Council,
and the Government of Canada through the Book Publishing
Industry Development Program.   Canada

TABLE OF CONTENTS

THANKS

Thanks to Jack David, Jen Hale, and Mary Bowness from ECW Press. A special thanks to Paul Zimic and the staff at The Academy; Claire Burton; Robyn Smith at *Ralph* Magazine in Australia; Tara "LJC" O'Shea and Robin Mayhall from Close Quarters Standby. A personal thanks goes out to family, friends, and colleagues at the North York Central Library for all their support, understanding, and friendship.

To Gil Adamson for everything.

And finally, to Luc Besson, the creator of Nikita.

"NUTHIN' FANCY, LUV; I'M AUSTRALIAN": PETA WILSON

It was a spring day in Sydney, Australia, when Karlene Wilson gave birth to her first child, a baby girl. Peta Gia Wilson was born November 11, 1970. Years later, on the talk-show circuit, Wilson found herself explaining the origin of her name — originally intended to be Pieta — more than once: "Well, it's not really an Australian name. In Italian it means 'pity,' and in Greek it means 'stoned and drunk.' We prefer the Australian version which was [that] I was named after Miss Australia 1970 [Peta Toppano, now an actress]."

Peta's father, Darcy, an army man, was not there when his daughter arrived. He was in the outback, and when the army said go, you went. Away in the "bush," word came to him that his child had been born, but by the time the child's name, "Pieta," reached his ears, it had become "Peter." He was the proud papa of a son! Nothing could make a father prouder, especially an Australian father. A boy to raise, to take fishing, to take sailing and to, maybe, one day, follow in a proud family tradition of military service. "Peter's" father, grand-father, and great-grandfather had all served in the army. "He came into town thinking he had a boy," remembers Peta. "It's actually a variation of Peter, Petra, or something, and my father turned it into Peta." A year after Peta was born, her mother gave birth to a boy, Rob, who did indeed follow in his father's footsteps and now drives 38-wheelers for the Australian army.

Australia is still a largely untamed country with a rugged terrain, virtually uninhabitable in parts, with the bulk of its population inhabiting larger towns and cities along the coastline. It is primarily a male-dominated society populated by strong men and by women who have to be just as strong to deal with the country and the men. The life of an army family is highly nomadic, and it was no different for the Wilsons. Darcy received a new posting every six months, so the family packed up and moved many times. It was a life that bred adaptability in the children and tested Karlene's strength regularly.

When the family eventually moved to a rural area of Papua New Guinea (PNG), where they would remain until Peta was nine, her mother raised her two young children without many amenities, often without running water or modern toilets. But she coped with whatever came her way (including Peta's nine-month bout of malaria in 1975) and gave the children a happy, free, and spirited childhood. Peta's mother became a strong role model for Peta as did her grand-mother, "Nana" White. These two women often discussed child rearing and the challenges of handling Australian men. Peta explains, "It's very Irish, my family. But oh, strong women. My grandmother used to say 'Well, if they get in the car you better get in the car with 'em. Pack the kids and go.' And Australian men maybe set the pace for Australian women because they're very strong. . . . So the Australian women are dealing with a strong animal there."

The family's years in PNG proved formative for Peta. Here her imag-ination blossomed, and she developed a spiritual connection with nature and animals that has never left her. There was no television or radio so Peta and her brother made up stories, went exploring, and became self-reliant. They spoke Pidgin English and lived the life of

Various scenes from Papua New Guinea *Clockwise from top left*: Coral reef and island off Madang coast; creek and forest between Menemango and Wemawa; Karkar Island; Baiyer River Valley; Port Moresby, the capital of PNG; waterfall between Kanabea and Menemango.

other children their age native to PNG. Peta remembers, "My brother and I were in the minority, we were the only white kids. I never felt prejudice from these people and I felt I learned so much about important things." She grew up thinking she would share these riches with others as a photojournalist for *National Geographic*. "I think native communities — I'm talking about small islands, not Africa — are misunderstood because they're feared, because they're unknown. But they have so much richness, so much, and I got a lot. So I always wanted to go to different tribes and go around the world photographing them and trying to tell the world about it."

Her love of photojournalism continues to this day, and she has filled her house with books and collections of photographs of people and places from around the world. As part of her preparation as an actor she uses animals as models for understanding character. "That's a great way to learn about people — watching animals," she says. "So I just watch the Discovery Channel every week, I watch animals, and then the bad guys and good guys in *Nikita* remind me of certain animals."

While she was growing up her connection to animals was also part of her family life. In fact, over the course of her youth her

A Gaiva pig, which is often eaten in PNG.

dad or mum, both animal lovers, also brought into the house a wild boar, a goat, cats, a great Dane (named Herman), tortoises, frogs, and blue-tongue lizards. It was all part of life on the island: "We'd take long walks through the rainforest and had lots of animals: a pet alligator, crocodiles, kangaroos. I remember it was the best time of my life."

Her father would often return home, after being away,

with some new creature to add to the menagerie. At one point the family lived across the river from the local village. Their yard was cut out of a cane field, and every morning the snakes and cane toads were cleared out so that Peta and Rob could play. After one absence Darcy Wilson brought home a baby crocodile just a couple of inches long and the story became the stuff of family legend.

Two baby crocs like the one Peta's family owned.

Peta tells the story animatedly: "We lived on the edge of a cane field, right? The houses are cut out. And two houses down there's this guy, [the] Lieutenant. . . and he's got this beautiful swimming pool, right? We're never allowed in it because we're the grommits ["riff-raff"] at the end of the street, and Dad's like a sergeant. We weren't in the pool, our pool's like half of a water tank cut in half, in New Guinea, everyone's gotta have one. So the pet crocodile is sitting in the pool one day, it rains. It rains heavy in New Guinea. [The rain] comes, the crocodile gets up in the middle of the pool, it gets out of the pool, gets in the neighbor's swimming pool. Seven o'clock in the morning you hear him getting up, stretching, the guy who'll never let us in the pool, gets up in the morning, doing his exercises and all of a sudden you hear, 'WILSON, GET THIS GODDAMN CROCODILE OUT OF HERE!' . . . And we came down there and it was attached to his finger in the pool."

Exotic animals also made their way into the Wilsons' cuisine. The children were sometimes minded by Aka, a woman from the local village who would feed them what some westerners might consider unusual fare. Peta has eaten crocodile burgers and snake meat and even owl. In the literal mind of a child, though, the experience was revisited with a twist. Three years old and finding herself a bit hungry, Peta spotted a dead owl: "I just thought, 'Oh, I've had that. Aka gave me that. Yummy, I'm hungry.' My mother was horrified." Of course, Karlene Wilson's reaction was understandable when one considers that Peta had found the owl in a latrine and her mother had discovered her little girl with feathers sticking out of her mouth.

Peta's mother also tried her hand at introducing animals into the family life. Tired of cutting the grass, she brought home a goat to do the job. The goat had a mind of its own, however, and, finding the grass not to its liking, it turned its attention to the laundry. On another occasion, taking her cue from other locals, Karlene decided the family would raise pigs. Why not save a bit of money and fatten up their own pigs for food? But mistakenly she brought home a wild boar, which is inedible, completely untamable, and uncatchable! After some hilarious chases through the house and yard, Mum and the kids gave it up as a lost cause.

Holidays meant visits with her grandparents in Australia. And it was here that Peta got her first introduction to television and American pop culture. *I Dream of Jeannie* quickly became a favorite for Peta, and her grandparents sent her home to PNG with hot-pink satin harem pants. The exotic outfit was a big hit, as were the scenes Peta acted out with her brother for their friends. Peta admits she was never really what you could call shy. Acting, singing, and performing came naturally, and she got an early start. When she was four years old she jumped onto the stage at the New Year's Eve party and entertained the gathering with a tap-dance. It was her first public performance and as Peta sums it up, "They couldn't get me off the stage." Four years later at a Christmas party the band failed to show up, and Peta again jumped onstage to sing and dance and this time got calls for an encore. Her mother teases, "She's been working the room since she was two." Peta elaborates, "According to my mother, I apparently came out of the womb like, 'I'm ready for my close-up, Mr. Fellini.'"

Sydney, Australia

Music was an important element of life in the Wilson household and Peta and her brother would lip-synch songs by Toto, Fleetwood Mac, Liza Minelli, and Barbra Streisand. After dinner they would put on skits and standup comedy routines and offer impersonations of family members. Peta took piano lessons, learned to tap-dance, and expanded her repertoire. Laughter was abundant and valued in the Wilson household and is evident in Peta the adult. Unlike her television alter ego, Wilson is quick to laugh and uses humor as a natural form of expression to build bridges between herself and strangers and to keep herself energized on the *La Femme Nikita* set.

The crew can never know what to expect when Peta appears on the set. "When I'm in the show, I tend to be a little bit of a boy most of the day, to keep open, keep me spontaneous. . . . I tend to be quite tomboyish, a little tough. I rough the crew up a little, I give them a bit of a hard time." She laughs. On her lunch breaks Peta works out with Canadian trainer Al Greene. She exercises, does some kick boxing, and will even do hand stands on the set between set-ups. "Usually I'm a little feisty after lunch. You know, I'll come back and the give the boys a bit of a rough and tumble, it helps me stay in character."

When Peta was nine, the family moved back to Australia. Her father continued to be transferred from location to location, and the family began its most intense period of upheaval. Peta attended nearly a dozen schools (usually girls' schools) but she maintained good grades and learned to make friends quickly and easily. Her outgoing personality served her well, and she proved to be highly adaptable. "I'd go to schools in these little outback towns. Some had five classes in one room. I'd only be there for six months at a time, so I had to make friends quickly. The first few days, I'd just watch whatever they were good at — sports, swimming — then, I'd venture in and get really good at it. That's how I'd fit in. Or I'd be the fool, the class clown, cheeky with the teacher. I entertained. I learned to act early out of necessity."

The transition was sometimes painful. She missed her friends in PNG and she missed the freedom that was her day-to-day life. As a child she had run through the jungle, played on the beach, swam in the ocean, and learned to climb palm trees. She led a natural life of freedom, connected to the natural world. The stricter Australian schools took some getting used to. She describes the contrast between her old life and her new one: "I came back to Australia . . . and it was traffic and cars and clique-y little groups. Free spirits were abundant in Papua New Guinea, and free-spiritedness in Australia in school is, 'She's a difficult child.'"

Sports become her passion. It wasn't just a way of fitting in, it was a way of excelling. And excel she did. She joined the netball team and while in high school she made the Australian National Team as its youngest member, distinguishing herself as the Most Valuable Player. These days, when being interviewed in North America, she frequently finds herself explaining the difference between netball and basketball, "In netball, you can't dribble the ball. You can't dribble and you can't run with it. Once you catch it, you've got to pass it. We've got the same court as basketball. It's a very tactical game and it's not as loose as basketball. You're only allowed to have [the ball] for three seconds."

She was also able to share several of her father's passions: motor-cycles, cars, and sailing. Darcy had been a motorcycle cop at one point and had an antique Norton, which Peta loved to ride. She learned how to fix cars and does much of the maintenance on her own to this day. She and her brother, Rob, had been sailing since they were ten. Their father had taken them to the smaller islands around PNG when they were young and once they were old enough he started them on lessons of their own. It was a way to spend time together and enjoy the water and the beauty of Australia.

It was also an opportunity for competition. Every year the National Corsair Championship was held, and Wilson's boat — the *Bewitched* — was entered with the youngest crew in the race (Peta, Rob, and three other children). Their Corsair, a racing boat, is also referred to as a Trailer Sailor because it is small enough to be towed on a trailer from the back of a car.

"My father was in command and I was the first mate. I worked the spinnaker. It was great. We were third across the line among five hundred boats. We capsized three times. And we were third over the line in the heaviest boat in the squadron by a lot. And we were the youngest crew. We also won the top-bottom trophy, which was a toilet seat. Because we capsized the most amount of times." Peta laughs. "It was my fault. I couldn't get the spinnaker up in time, so the wind kept pushing us over. That was really frightening, stuck in the water with this heavy boat and my furious dad." Still, by the end of the race they had won two trophies and they had done it together. That team spirit served her well while sailing and playing netball and would define her life as an actress in later years.

The single most significant event of Peta's childhood was her parents' divorce when she was just twelve. It split the family in two. Peta continued to live with her mother but her brother, Rob, left with her father. It was a difficult time for everybody, and for some time afterward Peta would sit on the garden fence and wait for her dad to come home. In fact, for the next three years she sent Valentines to

Bondi Beach, Sydney.

each of her parents, signing their names in the hope of generating a reconciliation.

She missed her brother, who had been her full-time childhood companion and whom she had defended by beating up anyone who picked on him. Family ties had been the one constant in a youth filled with change, and now that was gone. For a tomboy like Peta, the removal of a father figure placed an added strain on her ability to cope. Her mother's career as a caterer meant a lot of traveling, so Peta went to live with her grandparents in hopes of finding some stability. She buried her feelings of anger and loneliness.

Life with her grandparents was good. During the school year Peta devoted herself to her studies and her extracurricular activities. Her grandmother, Elizabeth, would wake her up early in the morning for swimming and netball, and after school she would take judo lessons. Every day she and her grandfather, Theo, would head down to the beach to fish, talk, and tell tall tales. A second emotional blow followed hard upon the first when Theo died, and Peta was left to deal with the loss of another male figure in her young life.

Growing up, Peta was a real tomboy. Her hair was short, she wouldn't wear a dress, and wanted to be called Pete — a family name, which sticks to this day. But by the time Peta was fifteen, Karlene decided it was time to smooth out some of her daughter's rough edges and to balance the masculine with a little of the feminine. She sent her for a few courses in "grooming and deportment." Not surprisingly, Peta did well. After all, she'd excelled at just about everything else she'd put her mind to. And the timing was right. She was becoming a woman.

The classes gave her confidence in herself physically at a time when most girls are particularly awkward. Peta still had no interest in boys — except as skate-boarding partners — but they were beginning to get interested in her. Her mother's business was doing well. Karlene was single again and was enjoying life, and she had bought herself a little British MG (a sports car). Peta describes her mother as beautiful and sexy and possessed of a flamboyant nature. Still struggling with her own emerging sexuality, she certainly didn't find it easy to reconcile her mother's: "I was very prudish until about the age of 16 or 17, then I realized it's okay to be feminine, it's okay to express your sexuality."

When her mother would come to pick her up at school, the strait-laced Peta, still trying to fit in with her Catholic-school girl-friends, would find herself flustered by her mother's obvious and unique qualities. Like most girls her age, she wanted *her* mother to be like everybody else's. And somewhere in her heart she still hoped her parents would get back together. Naturally these conflicts passed, and today it's Karlene who smiles to see her daughter in sexy, glamorous attire. And for Peta, those qualities that once evoked an adolescent embarrassment are part of what she prizes most dearly in her mother today.

Eventually the classes led to some modeling work. At first there were small jobs working as a runway model at the local shopping mall. With characteristic self-mockery she tells the story of her first job. "[It was] my first modeling job on a catwalk, like a Saturday morning job. I was feeling pretty fabulous, walking out there in a bathing suit. I get so excited and so overwhelmed [with] the audience I walk straight off the end of the catwalk and into the display swimming pool. I got back on the catwalk saturated [and] kept going."

In spite of the wet start and undeterred by mishaps, Peta continued to work and was soon scouted by an agent from a prominent Australian modeling agency. This was the same firm that had launched the early careers of Rachel Hunter and Elle MacPherson. She started getting work regularly for magazines, catalogues, and commercials. She finished high school and began working full time, traveling to Italy, Paris, and London. She used the job "as a passport to see the rest of the world." She would take a job, make some money, travel until the money ran out, and then take another job. It was an exciting life, she was meeting celebrities and having fun. But it was hard work, too, and Peta was happy to go home and share, with her mother and grandmother, her new clothes and her new experiences.

At the heart of it all Peta knew modeling was a business, that it was superficial, and that it wasn't enough for her. The knowledge was hard won. While she was still abroad she began to lose weight. At first it was hardly noticeable on her 5'10" frame but by the end of the year she had dropped 30 pounds and had gone from a healthy 140 to an extremely thin 110 pounds. She suffered from bouts of anorexia and bulimia. She was depressed and she wasn't sure why.

In the end Wilson feels it was a combination of a weariness with her career and the surfacing of unresolved conflicts she felt over her parents' divorce. She had been carrying that pain into her other relationships, too, including one with a fellow who followed her home to Australia from Italy and another with a hard-drinking musician. As she says, "Up to that point, any boyfriend I had lasted three weeks." She went home and confronted her parents with her buried feelings. She sought treatment and started to talk about it. With those lines of communication opened and with the love of her family, she felt the pain begin to slip away.

Peta had been making more money than the rest of her family put together, but she wasn't happy with her work. It was her outgoing nature and her sense of fun that landed her many of the jobs on the catwalks of Europe, but those same qualities were being smothered in a career where one is seen and not heard. She needed creativity and self-expression. However, she was hesitant to take up acting because she though it was nearly as narcissistic a pursuit as modeling. Originally she had thought to follow her dad into the army or make a life as an athlete. Even while she had been modeling Peta had considered other options. A cousin found her some work on a construction site. "I lasted about three days," she conceded.

In 1991 Peta stopped fighting the inevitable, packed up her things, and headed for the United States to study acting. She landed in New York and fell in love with the city, but when she became the target of an attempted mugging she reassessed the situation, bought herself a car — a 1957 Thunder-bird she calls Stella — and headed for Los Angeles. "I love old cars and I had ten thousand dollars in my pocket. I sort of lived out in my car and relied on the kindness of strangers, stayed in people's houses, and finally I found a drama school that was right for me. And I started to study and it was more for me. Acting wasn't so much, 'I wanted to be in movies.' I've got a lot of energy, I love to put it out there, so what a great job for me to do. Not only am I good enough for myself, I can play three or four different characters, as well, so it was more medicinal."

That journey of self-discovery and study of her craft took her to teachers like Arthur Mendoza from the Actors Circle Theater in Los Angeles and Tom Waits at TomCats Repertory Group and to Stuart Rodgers and Sylvia Gulado. She read, she watched, and she learned to push her ego out of the way and open herself to the truth: the truth of a scene, the truth of a character, and most importantly the truth within herself.

She became enthralled with the theater and particularly with Tennessee Williams. Her Australian accent started to soften, and she learned to do a very good Southern belle accent. Eventually she starred in a rep company production of Sam Shepard's *Fool for Love*. Interestingly, most of her work in school centered around vulnerable, "complacent, very sensitive, virginal characters." She credits this work with rounding out her skills. "When I came back to doing my strength, which is tough girls, I had a vulnerability worked into my craft."

Some might think that for a woman who was tired of being judged by her looks, she had chosen an odd profession. Hollywood is notorious for its consumption and disposal of pretty faces. Although Peta continued to model off and on over the years to pay the bills, she had no illusions about what she was facing. She continued to study, certain that in the end her talent would overshadow her beauty and convinced that there was no other way to achieve the career she wanted.

Her teachers, particularly Arthur Mendoza, continued to drive and inspire her. "He was so hard on me, it was a joke. He believed that I could have a career anyway, because if you're a pretty girl in L.A., you sort of can. But I said no, I want to be an actress! So he was harder on me than he was on any of the other students, and I'm so happy he was because I feel like I can really create characters now, and I'm not frightened of anything."

As her life as a drama student began to take root, so did her personal life. After kicking around from place to place, Peta finally rented a house with a girlfriend. Several months later she met Damian Harris, a young film director. She was 21 and he was 36, divorced, with a young daughter. They met at a party and she told him she was a Dutch clog dancer. In L.A., aspiring actresses are a dime a dozen, so Peta would make up stories about herself "because everyone asks you what you do. They come to that very quickly. One week, Daddy was a sheep farmer wanting to invest in movies. Then, I was a technical whiz for a software company. I used different accents. Or pretended I couldn't speak at all." They became friends. At first Peta was not interested in an older man with a daughter on the rebound from a divorce, but the relationship blossomed quickly. After three months they

Peta arrives at the 1997 *Cable Ace Awards* in a Valentino dress, with boyfriend Damian Harris.

moved in together and have been together ever since. She describes him as a poet, her dark prince, and a refined, intelligent artist.

In 1995, Peta landed a role in Rupert Wainwright's independent film *The Sadness of Sex*. The film, co-written by the director and New York author Barry Yourgrau, is based on Yourgrau's collection of short stories of the same name. The film was produced by L.A.-based but Canadian-owned Skyvision Partners and was shot, primarily in Toronto, over 12 days with a budget of $500,000. *The Sadness of Sex* is a collection of 15 vignettes that prominently features Yourgrau as the stories' narrator with Wilson playing "The Girl of His Dreams." The

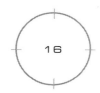
stories revolve around the author's musings about love, desire, and relationships. The director uses a wide range of visuals (everything from rock video parody to home video to film noir) and a soundtrack that includes music by Stewart Copeland and Cowboy Junkies, among others.

Defying categorization as either a romantic comedy or a surreal art film, the 85-minute piece drew mixed reaction from reviewers but earned thoughtful and positive reviews from *Los Angeles Times* writer Kevin Thomas and reviewer Andy Klein (*Cinemania Online*). Unfortunately, the film has received limited distribution. Its debut was in January 1996 at the Slamdance Film Festival in Park City, Utah, and turned it up at several other American film festivals until its limited theatrical release in April 1997. *The Sadness of Sex* made its Canadian debut at the Ottawa International Writer's Festival on September 14, 1998, playing to a full house of appreciative Yourgrau fans.

Also in 1995 Wilson was cast in another independent film called *loser*, written and directed by its star, Kirk Harris. Wilson plays Alyssha Rourke, the girlfriend of Jimmy Dean Ray (Harris). Shot over 13 days in El Monte, California, for just under $38,000, the film tells the story of a small-time drug dealer who considers the relationships in his life as he lies dying from a gunshot wound. Produced by Jack Rubio and Peter Baxter (who went on to become the head of the Slamdance Festival) with cinematography by Kent Wakeford (director of photography on such films as *Mean Streets* and *Alice Doesn't Live Here Anymore*), the film received excellent reviews after its award-winning premiere at Slamdance and during its 50-city theatrical release.

To flesh out her list of credits, Wilson also accepted a very small part in the 1995 release *A Woman Undone* starring Mary McDonnell as a woman accused of the murder of her husband. The film, which also starred Randy Quaid, Sam Elliott, and Benjamin Bratt, furnished Peta with one word of dialogue. *Naked Jane* (1995) also added to Wilson's résumé. In 1996, she landed a small part in an episode of the television series *Highlander*, shooting in Paris at the time. In the episode entitled "Promises," Wilson appeared as the Inspector. She has one scene: an interrogation of Duncan McLeod (played by the series' star, Adrian Paul), in which her voice appears to have been dubbed. That year she had another opportunity to try her hand at television work, in Paris, when she was cast in HBO's anthology series *Strangers*. She was in familiar company, as the episode was directed by Damian Harris. When Charlie Carner remade the 1971 cult classic *Vanishing Point* for television, Wilson was cast in the part played by Gilda Texter in the original film. The Nude Rider (Wilson) was clad in a bikini and renamed the Motorcycle Girl.

Working in Toronto on the set of *La Femme Nikita* was not Peta Wilson's first Canadian professional experience. In 1996, before being cast as Nikita, she headed north from L.A. to begin work on *One of Our Own*. Shot in Calgary over 22 days on a budget of just over $2 million, the film tells the story of two police detectives who pursue the kidnapper of the daughter of a deceased army buddy. Michael Ironside and Currie Graham star as the detectives who eventually uncover a weapons-trading scandal in this action film directed by David Winning.

Wilson beat out more than 100 other hopefuls to win the part of Corporal Jennifer Vaughn. She was, of course, an unknown at the time of shooting, but by August 1998, when the film was released theatrically, *La Femme Nikita* was finishing its second season. "No one knew who she was," says Bruce Harvey, the film's producer and owner of Calgary-based Illusions Entertainment Inc. "She came in and she caught our attention very quickly and held the whole audition. She has a very powerful personality and has a lot of sex appeal going for her. It was really exciting seeing her."

Wilson valued the opportunity to work with some outstanding talent: "I play a marine, an MP — I wanted to do it for the experience, to work away from home. It was very interesting working with Michael Ironside, and I really loved working with Marshall Bell and Frederick Forrest. When you're starting out, you take what you can get. The pot of gold is not at the end of the rainbow, it's the rainbow itself, in these kind of careers — it's the journey before you get there."

She enjoyed her time in Calgary, traveling to the mountains and going to sweat lodges. And it was here that she envisioned her dream to create a performing-arts school for underprivileged children. "It came to me in Calgary, and then the reality hit me that people wouldn't know who I was, and then in the course of five nights it came to me in a dream. And now I have the opportunity to do something like this for kids who need the opportunity. I want to give something back. Kids are the future. No matter who or what they are. Kids on the street could better express their inner voices in a positive way. That's my passion, I have to do that. It's why I'm here. Hopefully it will be something that people will come and lecture at, and teachers, other students, then take it back to their own country. It's a big dream."

Wilson studied in L.A. for six years. She landed a few parts, most of them small and most of them in smaller or independent productions. She continued to go to auditions for film work while supplementing her income with modeling work. She did well, usually ending up on the director's short list, but the process was disheartening. As she describes it, "I was getting sick of sitting on my butt, taking a number, then losing parts to big names."

She needed to practice her craft, and she decided to make the move to New York. "In the first six months I was in L.A. I got a couple of movie roles, but about six times I lost a part to a star. I said to my manager, 'Look, I don't wanna sit on my ass in L.A. and not do anything. I'd rather go to New York and do theater.' So my manager said, 'Just try TV.' Right away, I got offered three things: a sitcom on Fox, a Western at CBS, and *La Femme Nikita*."

Wilson's initial reluctance to audition for TV roles was motivated by a strong self-awareness. She knew her energy and personality were large and she feared they were a bit much for the small screen. Her theater training had prepared her to use her entire body to tell a story, not to limit herself to what a camera would catch in close-up.

Controlling that energy has resulted in a focused and powerful performance. And not just for Wilson. The same can be said of her fellow players who have all moved between the stage, film, and television. This reflects something that British actors have known for some time and that North American actors are beginning to learn: that the medium will not restrict a good performance — work is work. In North America there has been a prevailing snobbery about film work over television work, and the media are filled with stories about "upstart" actors who make the move from the small to the big screen. In the UK this distinction is irrelevant. A perfect case in point would be 1997's Mrs. Brown, a film made in England for television starring Dame Judi Dench, which showed theatrically in the United States and garnered her an Oscar nomination.

Wilson's manager, Michael Picone, convinced Peta that the experience would be beneficial and that she might learn something in the process. If she landed a part, at the very least, there would be new techniques to learn. So she went out to the auditions anyway, had fun and landed three roles on the first day. She credits her theater training and positive, no-nonsense attitude for such overwhelming and immediate success. She was so relaxed that she laughs remembering how her chatting was distracting the other actresses who were trying to prepare.

Joel Surnow auditioned more than 200 actresses for the part of Nikita. Wilson was the third one he saw: "She came in scruffy jeans and had a big [appendectomy] scar on her belly. She was really gnarly, hair flying in every direction. Afterwards, she sat on a chair . . . and became the most charming, chatty Australian girl." They liked what they saw immediately, and Wilson spent the day going from one meeting to another until, nine meetings later, she was finally ushered into an office packed to capacity with Warner Brothers executives. She began her scene with little more space to work in than the chair in which she was seated. She began the scene: Nikita, the street kid, awakens to find herself in Section instead of in her death-row bed. Disoriented, threatened, and angry she is like a trapped animal ready to attack. Wilson reached out and grabbed the basketball (covered in NBA autographs) belonging to the head of Warner Brothers and started bouncing it off the wall while she ran the scene for the startled executives.

"I did an audition where I just terrorized the office. I came in a mess, with no makeup on, in character like I was doing a play. After we did the audition, I acted like a normal person, which just blew them away," she remembers. "And then I drove out of the Warner Brothers car park in my 1973 Cutlass. So it was one of those kinds of stories."

Warner Brothers had already taken a risk on Nikita's story when they bought the rights to Luc Besson's original film creation to remake *La Femme Nikita* as *Point of No Return* with Bridget Fonda. But when Rod Perth, then head of the USA Network (a Warner Brothers company), received a script for *La Femme Nikita* from Joel Surnow, he was convinced that the film had potential as a television series. It didn't hurt that adapting for television a film that had become something of a cult hit made for a marketing advantage. "There you are, buried up on channel 39 or something and competing against the traditional networks with very lean resources," says Perth. "A project based on a feature gave me viewer awareness without putting a nickel behind marketing." Joel Surnow already had a successful track record as a writer for *Miami Vice* and as a producer for *The Equalizer*, among other things. It seemed natural that he be given the task of developing the series for the network.

In the July 17, 1995, issue of *Variety*, the leading US industry magazine, it was reported that the USA Network was developing the project with French production company Gaumont (whose credits include the highly successful *Highlander* and its spin-off *Highlander: The Raven*). It was announced at the semi-annual Television Critics Association press tour that in this version "Nikita will be a target rather than an assassin." Nearly a year later, in April 1996, *Variety* reported that *La Femme Nikita* was part "of a record $175 million commitment by USA for original programming." With a budget of $900,000 (not far from broadcast network standards for similar programming), La Femme Nikita became "the first big scale original series mounted by Warner Brothers directly for cable." And it was a business decision that paid off; by the end of the first season the "Sunday Night Heat" block (La Femme Nikita along with Silk Stalkings and Pacific Blue) had increased its ratings by 30 percent over the previous year. La Femme Nikita went on to become the highest-rated original drama on the network.

It took Wilson some time to decide to accept the Nikita role. She accepted the sitcom role she had been offered first. But a conflict with the lead actor, who came on to her, convinced her the job wasn't worth the hassle. Next she considered the Western. Her experience performing Tennessee Williams on stage and her rather good Southern belle accent argued in her favor. But the producers changed their minds, deciding she was younger than they wanted to cast for the part. The part ultimately went to someone with a name. (She has never said who got the role, nor what either show was called.)

During the Nikita audition, Wilson completely buried her Australian accent: "I came on sounding very American, a bit like Lauren Bacall and Kathleen Turner in one," she explains. "The producers told me to keep my accent, that it belonged in a series with an international flavor. In the audition, I had to show I could be an actress of many colors, that I could go from playing street urchin to Grace Kelly." She had been convincing, and the producers for La Femme Nikita continued to call, pressing her for a decision.

With characteristic forthrightness she honestly told them that she had gone to the audition to get some experience with auditions. She was uncertain she could handle the responsibility of a lead role in a series. And she wanted to be convinced that the spirit of Besson's original creation was not going to be exploited. Finally assured on the latter point and encouraged by her manager, her drama teachers, and friends, she accepted the part. She had nothing to lose and a lot of hard work ahead of her.

Nikita, the character, would go through a few changes before emerging in her television incarnation. Surnow faced a dilemma. How was he going to get American audiences to tune in each week to watch the show without sacrificing its dark core? "I felt the show wouldn't be worth doing if we couldn't preserve the raw complexity and sexuality of the film," he says. "I think it's more ruthless at the core than any show that I've ever done. I've done some tough shows. I did *Miami Vice* and *The Equalizer*, which had some really hard action, and I did the *Wiseguy* movie. But the protagonists in this show operate in a way that almost appears more villainous than your antagonists."

In a meeting that included the series' new star, Peta Wilson, Nikita's circumstances were reconceived to create a point of identification for an audience. Where Besson's title character had murdered a cop, this Nikita would be an innocent victim of circumstance: a woman who had stumbled across the back-alley homicide of a policeman and who, in struggling with the killer, had wrested away the murder weapon only to be discovered by police, knife in hand. Where the original Nikita was a drugged-out gang member, the television Nikita would be a homeless youth eking out a living on the streets after being thrown out of her home by her mother. Nikita's *raison d'être* would not be merely survival but her quest to retain her humanity in the face of the overwhelming and impersonal machine of Section One. Surnow explains, "The whole idea of a tortured soul is very important. You're dealing with a government operative who moves through a dangerous, violent world while trying to carve out and save a little piece of humanity for herself."

Having finally accepted the part, Wilson threw herself into the process of preparation in keeping with her theater school training. She hired and paid for the services of an ex-airborne ranger named Tirion Mortrell to train her in military and commando techniques. She learned how to handle a gun (break it down, load it, and fire it) firing over 800 rounds over the course of her training. She learned techniques of self-defense and break-and-enter techniques, which she practised on her own home. After six weeks of physical and mental training (including something Mortrell called "sensory intuition"), Wilson was dropped in an unfamiliar area of the city and required to evade her "opponents" in a war game designed to employ all her new training.

While she trained physically Wilson began the inner preparation for the character, ultimately creating a "bible" for Nikita, "six inches thick" (which she passed on to the series' department heads), filled with observations and theories about who the character was, where she had come from, how she'd stayed alive on the streets, and what motivated her. Wilson envisioned a girl whose birth had been an unfortunate mistake and whose mother had never let her forget that fact. In spite of a lifelong defense of her mother against an endless string of abusive boyfriends, Nikita was rejected by her alcoholic mother and forced to live on the street, unloved and unwanted.

Wilson theorizes, "Nikita slept up top above the world where it would be kind of safer. She took odd jobs to get herself by and survive. Sometimes she would steal food. I don't think she would steal food. She *was* a hustler; she'd hustle in pool halls and stuff. This was all in my head. She was sort of a hustler and would always collect odd pairs of sunglasses she would find and these became part of her . . . when she was deciding today what kind of character she would be in order to hustle the money she needed, her chamleonness [sic] would come out. She had no role model and didn't know who she was and where she should be. She didn't really fit into any group."

The actress also took trips to the zoo. Finding inspiration and insight into character in animals, she likened Nikita to a wild cat: "I'd say the role model was a panther. Cats generally are nice animals, but if you hurt them or you threaten them, they become deadly."

In spite of all the preparation, Wilson felt herself to be "very green" about the technical end of television production and started her first season "nervous and apologetic." She sought the help of co-star Roy Dupuis, who is quick to compliment her: "She learned quickly. She's very intelligent." Her experiences on the stage had prepared her for a different environment. In this new world of television there was no rehearsal period; in fact there were no read-throughs until the second season (a change Wilson requested). She was surprised when the staff in the office told her the reviews were in. Theater notices, yes. Film reviews, for sure. But television? She didn't realize television shows received reviews.

Continuity issues were another big surprise for the actress, who was used to performing a dramatic piece from beginning to end. In television, scenes are shot out of order, following logistical needs pertaining to the scheduling of cast members, location shooting, or set construction. Dramatic structure emerges in the editing room when all the smaller pieces come together. Wilson recalls, "When I started I was like, 'Holy hell, what am I doing?' I come from the theater. But now I've learned the techniques, it's harder to do than some fantastic play. There are so many things you've got to think about, like when the commercial break's coming." Of course, she has encountered some of the same conditions when shooting on film sets, but this time Wilson was the lead. She appeared in almost every scene, and her character was required to take an emotional journey over the course of each episode.

Still, producer Joel Surnow had no doubt that his casting decision was the right one. Part of his decision was informed by the very rawness with which the actress was struggling. Indeed there was a parallel, organic journey taking place for both the actress and her subject: "I didn't know anything about continuity, shooting out of sequence and stuff — I had had limited film and television experience. You've got to learn that, it's an art in itself. As I was adjusting to the medium, so was the character adjusting to her environment." She adds, "I hope I'm green for the rest of my life, so there's always a surprise, you're always learning. When I'm not green, I won't be doing this anymore — I'll be farming peanuts on a peanut farm or something."

Peta at home with her Nana.

This sense of personal balance, good training, hard work, a lot of laughter, and plenty of support from colleagues and family saw her through the early days of the production. Far from her home in L.A. and her family in Australia, Wilson encouraged visits from her mother, her brother, and her father to the set and to the city. Her Nana even came for an extended stay, living with Peta in her Toronto apartment and offering the same love and stability she'd given her granddaughter after Peta's parents divorced.

Eager to do her own stunt work, Peta quickly learned from the producers that insurance restrictions would prevent her from doing so. Obviously, if the lead actress were incapacitated the production would grind to an expensive halt. Her training had not gone to waste, though. Wilson took on all the physical work she was allowed: running, jumping, climbing, and fighting. However, early in the first season she learned the wisdom of letting her stunt double do the riskier work: "I got a concussion doing a stunt where I was supposed to be thrown against a tree. The director wanted me to really 'feel the tree.' The stuntman was helping me out, shall we say, and I caught the tree at ten miles an hour. I worked the rest of the day, then had a CAT scan." But not before she had called "cut" and stumbled into the woods to throw up and collect herself.

The incident didn't slow her down for long, nor did it curb her spirit of adventure. By the beginning of Season Two she was doing most of her own fight scenes. A typical day of shooting (for "Last Night") was described by a journalist: "Nikita dashes across a square after someone she thinks is the missing little girl and gets knocked out by a nasty thug. For ten different takes, Wilson gets conked over the head ten different ways. (The actress is constantly consulting Mic [Jones], the stunt coordinator, to make sure she's passing out realistically; she does most of her own stunts, including all the fights.) Finally the director yells "cut" and calls for a break. And even though Wilson has been running, punching, and falling for three straight hours on a bone-chilling cold spring day, she doesn't do the star thing and retreat to her trailer. Instead she hangs outside, yakking with the hair and makeup people, horsing around with the cute crew boys and strolling over to talk to the throng of kids who are hoping to get her autograph." In Season Three's "Someone Else's Shadow" she tackled her fear of heights and performed a three-story dive that was intercut with the stunt woman's eighteen-story jump.

Wilson rose to the challenges of being the star in a hit series. As the lead, she was very much the center of activity and atmosphere on the set. Each episode takes seven days to shoot; with a daily schedule of seven to ten pages, shooting could run as long as 17 hours. With the shoot running from October to May the crew experiences the harsh Canadian winters firsthand. The long hours quickly led to a strong sense of camaraderie on the set, with Wilson at its center with her raucous sense of humor, whirlwind energy, and extroverted personality.

And Wilson is not the only clown on the set as bloopers (available at the show's official Web site as downloadable clips) will attest. Dupuis, in particular, has a wicked sense of humor and enjoys playing practical jokes designed to relieve tension. One blooper shows Michael

Peta hams it up with guests at the 1998 Gemini Awards in Toronto.

making his usual cool approach to an enemy-occupied building; instead of pulling out his usual assault weapon he enters armed with — Super Soakers! The director and crew audibly break up off camera.

A team player in her youth, Wilson remains one as an actress, as do the rest of the cast and crew. There is no other way to put together a show of this quality in such a short time. It is also interesting to note that as the actors grew more comfortable with their parts and the writers wrote to their cast members' strengths, an ensemble approach began to emerge. Surnow explains, "In the beginning we were trying to sell her. Now we are more involved in all the characters. The whole idea of Section One has become a bigger deal than it was at the beginning. At the beginning we were dealing with [Nikita saying], 'Oh, my God, I'm stuck in this organization, what do I do now?' Now it's, 'I'm in the organization. I have moral issues about certain things I have to do, but we are all part of the team.'" This kind of growth is a strength of the production as a whole and fans see this. It was very possible early on that an action show with a beautiful female lead could have coasted on an established formula, but this one hasn't and it's a testament to the creativity of everyone involved in the production.

Balancing the creative side of show business with its commercial aspect, Wilson committed herself to promoting the show on many of her days off. Unlike many actors who prefer to opt out of the business side of the job, Wilson sees it as part of what she was hired to do. "I feel like a saleswoman," she says. "I feel like I'm out there — we've got this huge conglomerate, right — it's like a big building — and everyone else is working on it. Without the tiler, the painter, the plumber, we have no building. But guess what? I'm the saleswoman. So they build the whole thing and make it look really great. And I get out there, and I'm the one who sells it. So I'm on *Leno*."

In fact, Wilson has appeared at least once on nearly every major talk show in Canada and the United States. She has adorned the covers of dozens of entertainment, fashion, fitness, women's, and men's magazines in North America, Australia, and Europe working with photographers like Herb Ritts, David LaCapelle, Naomi Kaltman, and Tony Notarberardino. She was chosen by Bob Guccione Jr. for the cover of the premiere issue of his new magazine *Gear*, and she was hired as the spokesperson for an estimated $20 million campaign for Bally Total Fitness in 1998. She has made both "The Best Dressed" and "The Worst Dressed" celebrity lists within months of each other. Peta has also lent her name to fund-raising activities for the National Alliance of Breast Cancer Organizations, for Fashion Cares, and been honored by *Cosmopolitan* magazine as one of the "12 women who rocked our year" in 1998. The list goes on.

In spite of a generally sensible attitude toward the job, she did not find herself fully prepared for the onslaught of personal attention. Initially she says it was "a kick" to be recognized at the airport or in a restaurant and asked for an autograph. But soon her private time was not her own and she admits to making some mistakes on the homefront. She got, as she describes it, "a little bratty," and her beloved Nana headed back home for a break. "She's going to stay with me again. It was a great thing to have her there, but [the stress of publicity] became much more and I wasn't appreciating my grandmother as much as I should have been. So, I've smartened up and she's on her way."

At times it has all been a bit overwhelming but, innately leery of the pitfalls of the narcissistic aspects of her own profession, and armed with an eye to the bigger picture of what she hopes will be a lifelong career, she has resisted making many of the mistakes made by more experienced performers. Once again she credits her family and her upbringing in PNG and Australia for the perspective and values that have seen her through the challenges. "When you're an Australian army brat nothing much intimidates you. This all could be finished tomorrow. So I'm not going to waste my time being nervous and freaked about it." She adds, "I feel like a surfboard rider and I didn't know how to surf in the beginning and all of a sudden I stood up and I'm riding this fantastic wave and it's looking like it's going to go on forever. But I realize it could crash any second, so I'm going to enjoy the wave while I'm on it."

One aspect of all this newfound attention that continues to puzzle Wilson is the idea that she is some kind of a role model. But she is aware of the effect such a strong female role has in the minds of viewers. "Of course, I don't think women would necessarily want to do what Nikita does, but I do think they like the fact that she is a strong person who can stand up for herself. And I also think they like the fact that while there are some things she must do if she is to survive, she will not exchange her soul for survival."

But Peta remains adamant that her job as an actress is to act, to find and tell the truth about a character, and to serve a story to the best of her abilities. "I try not to think about [being called a role model]. That's not really an actor's job, it's just to do their job and act, and be conscious and aware of things going on around them. To make a difference in the roles they play." She adds with typical candor, "I'm not a bloody role model, I'm just an army brat from

Australia who had a dream and worked really hard and achieved it." She hopes if she can offer any inspiration to fans it is for them to find out what makes them special, set their goals, and work hard to achieve them.

Peta is concerned about the violence in the show, but is certain that the audience will see it for what it is and see it in its context of entertainment, not reality. Wilson does not own a gun nor will she allow one in her home. She is quick to point out that although Nikita has learned how to kill, she does so to survive and to defend those who cannot defend themselves. She is proud that her character acts as the conscience of Section and although it can be fun to *pretend* to "kick butt," the violence can take its toll on the actor behind the persona: "Sometimes it seeps into my own life, and I say, 'Oh god, I've got to go hurt someone again?' Sometimes I get sick or really tired or beat up or I cry a lot because the character's been going through stuff, and your body doesn't know 'We're acting now,' you know? You might be acting, but your body can really tell no difference."

Many critics agree that one of the show's unique strengths is its portrayal of violence with a conscience. In the *New York Times*, Margy Rochlin discussed the impact of having female leads such as Peta Wilson, Sarah Michelle Gellar of *Buffy the Vampire Slayer*, and Brook Langton of *The Net* explore issues of violence. She quotes *The Net*'s executive producer Patrick Hasburgh: "Anyone can write a tough guy. Bringing a female sensibility to that kind of character expands it ten times. There's a kind of truthfulness to the violence and a sense of how painful it really all is." Rochlin comments, "In this way, Gellar, Wilson, and Langton inhabit three of the most complex and unusual female characters on television."

Some critics point to *La Femme Nikita*'s allure as a "guilty pleasure." The *Village Voice*'s Tom Carson sees the show as "a funhouse mirror of the dystopic '90s workplace." Carson points out that although the series is clearly an "empowerment fantasy," it is also one "about feeling enslaved." His astute analysis continues, "On *Nikita*, this

A sweet-lip fish, the namesake of Peta's production company.

conundrum's right before our eyes — in the contrast between Peta Wilson's physical prowess and her trapped face. In a smart touch, she's been given the wan home life and drab digs of your typical office drudge, and it's also funny that, as much as Nikita resents being miscast in this line of work, she's still anxious to measure up; just like more conventional young professionals, she's scared of being found out as a fraud."

Wilson sums it up nicely. "People love the show because it's addictive, fast-moving eye-candy — with a conscience." It is this conscience, perhaps, that most interests the fans, as Section plays out one impossible ethical dilemma after another, with Nikita as the audience's point of identification.

Now that Wilson is, as she would put it, "a dot on the map," she has begun to look to the future. She is pursuing her dream to build a school for the performing arts for underprivileged children. To this end, she and her best friend and business partner, Jasper Sceats (son of Jonathan Sceats, who supplies La Femme Nikita with its signature sunglasses), have formed a company called Psycht, which will sell accessories such as sunglasses, watches, running shoes, and backpacks. Moneys raised will fund the school and support her new film production company, Sweet Lip Productions.

Sweet Lip Productions (so named because as a child the "sweet-lip" was her favorite fish) has a couple of projects in development. One is a documentary about Wilson's favorite playwright, Tennessee Williams, and the other is a Romeo and Juliet-style tale tentatively titled Garden in the Night. Her ambition is to create possibilities for herself and other actresses by producing projects that include the kind of roles for women that are so rare in Hollywood.

Spring 2000 saw the premiere of Wilson's first lead in a feature film, *Mercy*, directed by Damian Harris and based on the book by David Lindsay. Shot in Toronto in 1998, the film also stars Ellen Barkin, Julian Sands, and Wendy Crewson. Barkin plays a police detective and Wilson her chief suspect in a series of brutal killings. In the meantime, Peta's energy is being poured into *La Femme Nikita*. During breaks she returns to drama class to keep up her "chops."

Determined to balance her private and public life and realistic about the journey she has only just begun, Wilson aspires to attain the longevity and skill of one of her professional role models, Gena Rowlands. "I've learned a lot from doing this show, technically," she says. "Combine that with my theater training; I hope I've got a pretty good instrument. I think actors are like a piano. The more you train, the more you learn — you've got more keys to play with. At the moment, I've got, like, five keys. I'm playing a song with five notes. But I think as you get older and more experienced, sooner or later you're playing the whole piano."

Filmography:

Mercy, 1999; *One of Our Own*, 1998; *Naked Jane*, 1995; *The Sadness of Sex*, 1995; *A Woman Undone*, 1995; *loser*, 1995

Television (TVM-Television Movie):

La Femme Nikita, 1997– ; *Vanishing Point* (TVM), 1997; *Strangers*, 1996; *Highlander*, 1996

THE OTHER OPERATIVES

Roy Dupuis

Actor Roy Dupuis plays Michael, Nikita's trainer and mentor on La Femme Nikita. Although for many English-speaking fans this may be the first exposure to this Canadian actor, Dupuis has been working since 1986 in theater, film, and television in his native French tongue as one of Quebec's leading actors and biggest celebrities.

Born in Montreal April 21, 1963, Dupuis was raised in Amos, a small town in the Abitibi region of northern Quebec. Dupuis grew up with an older sister, Roxanne, and a younger brother, Roderick. With only one year between them, the three children were close, especially the boys. Roy and Roderick were nearly inseparable when young, so much so that they would sometimes be mistaken for one another around town.

The house in Amos backed onto a forest and young Roy was happiest playing in the woods and building treehouses. He was shy and introspective, but loved sports, particularly ice hockey. Athletic from an early age, Roy joined the hockey club and the swim team. He took karate for a year, when he was seven, and in school he played basketball and volleyball and joined the track and field team.

His father, Roi, came from a working-class family. His first job was in the mines; then he loaded trucks, and eventually he got a job selling meat for Canada Packers. Roi was an excellent hockey player who once aspired to a professional career. Although Roy describes his father as the authoritarian of the family, he does remember his dad teaching him to skate and swim at the age of three.

His mother, Ryna, née Thifeault, grew up with a rich heritage that gave her nobility and pride. Her father, Yvanneau, was a cook and her mother, Liane, was a musician who could play virtually any instrument. Roy remembers that his grandmother also had a mechanical aptitude, a knack for fixing just about anything from a toaster to a radio.

Ryna taught piano and balanced Roy's physical training with artistic pursuits. She enrolled him in cello lessons, which he took five days a week for seven years. Recently Dupuis took up his cello again and incorporated a short piece in a third-season La Femme Nikita episode, "Gates of Hell." As a teenager, he played guitar and sat in with friends in a local band from time to time.

When he was eleven, the family moved to Kapuskasing in northern Ontario. It was a big change for the boy, who spent the next three years learning to speak English in spite of the area's large French-speaking population. The biggest change in his young life came three years later, when his parents divorced. His mother took the three children and moved to the Montreal suburb of Sainte-Rose, and the split was so traumatic that Roy has rarely seen his father since.

Montreal was something of a revelation to a teenager from rural Quebec and Ontario. The Métro (subway) took him from one end of the city to the other for a single fare, and the city was alive with art, music, and culture. It's one of the most exciting and culturally diverse cities in North America, and Roy took to it like a fish to water.

Although he had participated in school plays, once playing the fox in the play *Le Petit Prince* by Saint-Exupéry, he had never considered a career in acting. He loved movies and would stay up on weekends with his mother, a fellow night owl, watching old classics. In high school he had many friends in the drama program but he was drawn to the sciences; he wanted to know how things worked and was intrigued by the natural world.

But everything changed in a series of now famous coincidences and accidents. A friend took him to see Ariane Mnouchkine's three-hour film *Molière*. Dupuis, seventeen, was enthralled by the man, by his era and by his work. The next day he dropped his physics course and picked up a class in drama.

To fulfill his diploma requirements he was asked to rehearse and perform a scene. Still inspired by Molière, he chose a scene from *La Malade Imaginaire* (*The Imaginary Invalid*), a Molière play usually studied at a post-secondary level. The scene was a success and caught the attention of his teachers and fellow students. Six months later, the drama department presented the entire play with Dupuis and his class, recruiting drama students from other schools and musicians from the city for the performance.

Dupuis's best friend, Michelle, was readying for her auditions for L'Ecole National du Théâtre du Canada (the National Theater School of Canada) when her partner dropped out. It was Roy's birthday, and as part of his present she gave him the application and invited him to come with her to audition. Their appointments were on the same day, so they decided to prepare a piece together. The competition was daunting, with nearly two thousand applicants and only 16 places, but the audition went so well that Dupuis was offered one of the coveted places in the program. (Michelle won a place the following year.) But when it came time to process his application, it was clear from the photograph submitted that Roy was not the Stephan Labelle he had claimed he was. (For starters, Stephan was black.) Director Michele Rossignol discovered the deceit but allowed Roy to fill in a new application and enter the program anyway.

Scholarships and loans paid for some of his school fees, but Dupuis also had an assortment of part-time jobs to make ends meet. And so began one of the happiest and challenging periods in his life. For the next four years, he studied drama and movement, theater and poetry, and took advantage of the six professional directors who would arrive each year to instruct the students in different schools of acting and enlighten them about living and working as artists.

Dupuis cites his encounter with Armand Gatti as one of the most influential events of his artistic life. Gatti was an Italian writer who moved to France when he joined the Resistance in World War Two. Writing in French, Gatti took seven years to create a piece called *Opera Avec Titre Long*, about the Germans who fought Hitler and were imprisoned and executed for joining the Resistance. The playwright chose the National Theater School and its students to debut the play. Gatti taught Dupuis that theatrical activity happens during rehearsals. Here decisions on how to move and how to say your lines are made, and the performance is the result of that process.

In the spring of 1986, Dupuis took part in the first of the now annual "General Auditions" at the Théâtre de Quat'Sous. These highly important auditions function like an actors' showcase to give young graduates and professional directors exposure to one another. Newly graduated, Dupuis began work immediately in a production of *Harold et Maude* (adapted from the movie of the same name) that toured Acadia for La Compagnie de Viola Légère.

Later that year, Dupuis landed his first serious leading role in Jean-Marc Dalpé's *Le Chien* for the Théâtre Nouvel-Ontario in Sudbury. It is a role that remains close to his heart, and he has often spoken of bringing it to the screen. The play toured to Ottawa and Montreal, making its English-language debut in Toronto.

Dupuis continued to work in theater in such plays as Shakespeare's *Romeo and Juliet* and Sam Shepard's *Fool For Love*, and he took small parts in films such as *Exit 234* and *Jesus of Montreal*. In 1990, four years after graduating from theater school, Dupuis made a decision that would change his life dramatically. He turned down an eight-month contract to appear on the Paris stage in Genet's *Haute Surveillance* and accepted the role of Ovila Pronovost in the television miniseries *Les Filles de Caleb*. He had been spotted by the series' director, Jean Beaudin, when he performed *Romeo and Juliet* at the Théâtre du Monde in 1989.

The show was an enormous hit in Quebec, drawing four million viewers each week — about eighty percent of the viewing audience. Dupuis's life ceased to be his own very quickly. He became a sex symbol overnight, and the Quebec tabloids reported his every move. He was still a young man and he was growing up in the limelight. He soon became known as a drinker and a club-goer. His every move was reported, analyzed, and judged. It became impossible for him to move about unrecognized in Montreal or anywhere else in Quebec. Besides the loss of privacy, he lost the anonymity an actor requires. Much of the actor's art lies in observation, watching people and how they behave. When he became the observed, it was impossible for him to study others freely.

Dupuis went on to dub his role into English for the English-language version of the series, *Emily*, and to reprise the role in 1993 in the follow-up series *Blanche*, which drew three-and-a-half million viewers a week. Before working on *Blanche* he joined the cast of *Scoop*, another television series, for a couple of seasons and boosted their ratings to 3.8 million viewers. After the excellent writing of *Les Filles de Caleb* and the rigors of taking his character, Ovila, from a young teen to a middle-aged man, his role as Michael Gagne in *Scoop* was not overly challenging. The actor grew restless and in 1994 returned to the theater in another Shepard play, *True West*.

Thirty days in 1992, however, marked a high point in Dupuis's artistic life. Three days before joining *Scoop* he wrapped on the film version of *Being at Home with Claude*. René-Daniel Dubois's play had had successful runs in Montreal and London, and garnered its lead — Lothaire Bluteau — great acclaim. When Jean Beaudin got the job to direct the film version, he cast Dupuis as Yves, the male prostitute who kills his lover at the height of passion. The film features an astounding and violently beautiful opening sequence shot in stark black and white. Dupuis spent a month researching his part in Montreal's gay district. He lost 25 pounds for the role in a successful effort to feminize the lines of his body. The film was a critical success, and a personal one, as well. Dupuis still singles out this performance as his best. Between Yves and Ovila, Dupuis spent two years winning one award after another for his work.

In 1994, Dupuis was set to break into the North American market. He starred in *Million Dollar Babies* opposite Celine Bonnier as Oliva Dionne, father to the Dionne quintuplets. The four-hour mini-series was broadcast simultaneously in Canada on CBC and in the United States on CBS. Two years later he made his American film debut in *Screamers* opposite Peter Weller as the Shakespeare-spouting Becker (the Shakespeare was Dupuis's idea). The sci-fi film, based on a story by Phillip K. Dick, did not become an overnight success but it did lead to more work in the United States, such as an unsold pilot opposite Kelly McGillis called *Dark Eyes*.

Finally in 1996, after several more French and American productions in theater, film, and television — including a small part in *Easy Money* in which he gets killed by his idol Marlon Brando! — Dupuis auditioned for the part of Michael in *La Femme Nikita*. He has said that he does not have a plan for his career mapped out but that he takes each role primarily because of the people involved. If he clicks with them then he takes the job. It was no different with *La Femme Nikita*; when he and Peta did their scene at the audition they hit it off right away. There was an instant chemistry between them, and it shows on the screen.

Working on *La Femme Nikita* has meant a substantial commitment for the actors involved. The show shoots for eight-and-a-half months a year, from October to June, and the actors sign the standard five-year contract. A typical day for Dupuis means waking up between 5:30 and 6:30 a.m., a quick shower, and a ride to the studio. A shooting day can be anywhere from 12 to 18 hours but typically it is about 14 to 15 hours. The shoot runs Monday to Friday, and every Friday night Dupuis flies to Montreal and then travels for another hour to spend the weekend at home.

Home is an 1840s farmhouse on fifty-four acres of land, which Dupuis bought in 1996 after a six-year search. The acreage is divided between 30 acres of woodland and 24 acres of field, and Dupuis has plans to excavate a two-acre swamp and turn it into a lake. Renovations to the house have been slow, but that's according to plan, says Dupuis. Like his uncle, he plans to make the farm his life's work and his legacy for his children.

There are two buildings on the property. The main building is a wooden structure with a stone basement. The second building dates back to 1870. The kitchen was the first area of the house to receive an overhaul. Dupuis built an oak porch and has started planting trees. The farm has become his safe haven, a place where he can read, walk in the woods, and look at the stars.

His club days are over, and he's been sober since 1995, having "given up thirst for lucidity." His favorite way to spend time is with his longtime girlfriend, Celine Bonnier, a few friends and his dogs. He loves to cook, work on the house, and listen to music. A self-confessed audiophile, he takes great pride in his sound system and has a large and eclectic collection of music. He continues to enjoy athletic pursuits such as cross-country skiing, sky-diving, boxing, and golf.

When his tenure with *La Femme Nikita* is over Dupuis plans to distance himself from television for a while and seek roles in film. He also hopes to work with Bonnier to produce and direct a documentary. His participation in a documentary about legendary hockey player Maurice "Rocket" Richard has recently concluded and may have inspired this new ambition. Dupuis will continue to challenge himself with new roles and new situations, true to his credo that his job as an actor is to serve the writer and director with his imagination, his conscience, his body and soul.

Filmography:

Hemoglobin, 1997; *Aire libre*, 1997; *J'en suis!*, 1997; *L'Homme idéal*, 1996; *Waiting for Michelangelo*, 1996; *Screamers*, 1995; *C'était le 12 du 12 et Chili avait les blues*, 1994; *Cap Tourmente*, 1993; *Entangled*, 1993; *Being at Home with Claude*, 1992; *Le Marché du couple*, 1990; *Jésus du Montréal*, 1989; *Comment faire l'amour avec un nègre sanse se fatiguer*, 1989; *Le Grand Jour de Michael Tremblay*, 1989; *Dans le ventre du dragon*, 1989; *Sortie 234*, 1988; *Les Enfants de la Rue*, 1987

Television:

La Femme Nikita, 1997– ; *Urgence* (TVM), 1996; *Dark Eyes* (TVM), 1995; *Million Dollar Babies* (mini-series), 1994; *Blanche*, 1993; *Scoop* II, 1993; *Scoop*, 1992; *Les Filles de Caleb*, 1990

Matthew Ferguson

Matthew Ferguson makes his home on Toronto Island, where he was born and raised. With a population of about 700 people, it is one of the city's most unique communities. When he was five, Matthew got his first exposure to political activism when he joined his neighbors as they successfully stopped developers' bulldozers from turning the island into a park.

Educated in Toronto, he is a graduate of the Claude Watson School for the Performing Arts. At the age of 16 he made a notable theatrical debut in the Theater Plus production of *Geometry, in Venice* as Morgan Moreen, for which he was nominated for a Dora Mavor Moore Award for Best Featured Actor. Ferguson made the move to film in 1992 with *On My Own* with Judy Davis and has garnered acclaim for his work in the form of three Genie Award nominations for his film work in *Eclipse*, *Lilies*, and *Love and Human Remains*.

He developed one of his more unusual skills when he became a stilt walker with the theater group Shadowland and their sister company Swizzle Stick, who perform at Toronto's Caribana Festival. And he learned a Northern Irish accent for a small part in *The Long Kiss Goodnight*: he gave the long kiss good-night that ended up on the cutting room floor, leaving audiences to ponder the meaning of the film's title.

Moving with ease between television, stage, and screen, Ferguson won the part of Seymour Birkoff in *La Femme Nikita* in 1996. His first continuous television role has meant another nomination: this time Canada's Gemini Award nomination for his performance in the episode "Noise."

A love of chocolate is about the only thing he shares with his cynical, agoraphobic television alter ego. Ferguson is a self-confessed sports nut who plays hockey, soccer, golf, and tennis. He is a member of a dragon-boat crew, and he plays for the *La Femme Nikita* hockey team opposite other local production teams. He also loves music, books, and gardening.

Ferguson frequently cites Tom McCamus as a major influence on his professional life. McCamus was his mentor in his first profession-ally staged production. (McCamus also starred in *I Love a Man in Uniform*, in which Ferguson acted, and recently co-starred with Alberta Watson in *The Sweet Hereafter*.)

On the set of *La Femme Nikita*, Ferguson's schedule often meshes with those of Don Francks and Eugene Robert Glazer, and the three men spend much of their off-camera time together.

Filmography:

Uncut, 1997; *The English Patient*, 1997; *Lilies*, 1996; *Billy Madison*, 1995; *The Club*, 1994; *Eclipse*, 1994; *Searching for Bobby Fischer*, 1993; *I Love a Man in Uniform*, 1993; *Love and Human Remains*, 1993; *On My Own*, 1992

Matthew Ferguson

Television:

La Femme Nikita, 1997– ; PSI Factor, 1996; The Deliverance of Elaine (TVM), 1996; Harrison Bergeron (TVM), 1995; Life with Billy (TVM), 1994; Lives of Girls & Women (TVM), 1994; Material World, 1990; Top Cops, 1990

Don Francks

Don Francks was born and raised in Vancouver, British Columbia. He began his acting career at the age of 11 in a stage play called The Willow Pattern Plate. He knew immediately that he wanted to act and sing.

B
I
O
G
R
A
P
H
Y

Don Francks sings jazz with the band at the 1999 Close
Quarters Standby convention.

As a young man he sang on radio programs, and by 1954, he was
acting in variety shows and dramas for television and writing docu-
mentaries and public-affairs specials. His work took him across the
country. In 1966 he landed a job in the United States as the lead in
the NBC series *Jericho*. Two years later, he made his feature film debut
acting and singing with Fred Astaire and Petula Clark in *Finian's
Rainbow*. In 1980 and 1981 Francks received ACTRA Awards for Best
Dramatic Performance for his work in *Drying Up The Streets* and *The
Phoenix Team*.

In the past 30 years, Francks has starred in innumerable television, film, and theater projects and has lent his unique voice to
hundreds of commercials and animated series, including *Beetlejuice*

Matthew Ferguson and Don Francks

and *Inspector Gadget*. Francks performs frequently in jazz festivals, has made several jazz albums, and is currently recording a new CD tentatively titled *Jazzsong*.

Francks lives in Toronto with Lili Red Eagle, his wife of more than 30 years. They have two children, actress Cree Summer and a son, Rainbow Sun. Francks also goes by the name Iron Buffalo and spent many years living on a reserve with his family. He has a lifelong devotion to the ideals of "world peace, the elimination of hunger, the cleanup of global pollution, a greater understanding of the environment, and humankind's independence."

Like *La Femme Nikita* co-star Peta Wilson, he has a passion for collecting cars and a love of motorcycles. In Francks's case the collection consists of 12 antique automobiles, mostly Model T Ford racing cars from 1912–27, and several Harley-Davidsons.

Don Francks stars as Walter in *La Femme Nikita*, a munitions and weapons expert with a knack for surviving the ruthless world of Section One. His warmth and humanity are unique and he acts as a friend, advisor, and touchstone for Nikita.

Filmography:

Dinner at Fred's, 1999; Summer of the Monkeys, 1998; Bogus, 1996; Harriet the Spy, 1996; Heck's Way Home, 1996; Johnny Mnemonic, 1995; First Degree, 1995; Paint Cans, 1994; Married To It, 1993; The Big Town, 1987; Terminal Choice, 1985; Rock & Rule (voice), 1983; My Bloody Valentine, 1981; Heavy Metal (voice), 1981; Fast Company, 1979; Riel, 1979; Fish Hawk, 1979; Summer's Children, 1979; Drying Up the Streets, 1978; McCabe & Mrs. Miller, 1971; Finian's Rainbow, 1968; Drylanders, 1963; Ivy League Killers, 1959

Television:

La Femme Nikita, 1997– ; Early Edition, 1996; Heart: The James Mink Story (TVM), 1996; The Conspiracy of Fear (TVM), 1996; A Vow to Kill (TVM), 1995; Degree of Guilt (miniseries), 1995; Hostile Advances: The Kerry Ellison Story (TVM), 1996; The Possession of Michael D. (TVM), 1995; Madonna: Innocence Lost (TVM), 1994; Small Gifts (TVM), 1994; The Diviners (TVM), 1993; Kung Fu: The Legend Continues, 1992; X-Men (voice), 1992; Quiet Killer (TVM), 1992; Cadillacs and Dinosaurs, 1991; The Road to Avonlea, 1990; On Thin Ice: The Tai Babilonia Story (TVM), 1990; Labor of Love (TVM), 1990; The Christmas Wife (TVM), 1988; Hot Paint (TVM), 1988; Alf Tales (voice), 1988; Captain Power and the Soldiers of the Future (voice), 1987; Starcom: The U.S. Space Force (voice), 1987; Ewoks (voice), 1985; Countdown to Looking Glass (TVM), 1984; Inspector Gadget (voice), 1983; 984: Prisoner of the Future (TVM), 1982; Seeing Things, 1979; The Littlest Hobo, 1979; Jericho, 1966; Mission: Impossible, 1966; The Wild, Wild West, 1965; The Man from U.N.C.L.E., 1964; The Virginian, 1962; R.C.M.P., 1960

Eugene Robert Glazer

Eugene Robert Glazer was born and raised in Brooklyn, New York. He confesses he originally had no drive to enter the acting profession, and so he began a career on Wall Street trading securities. But when his father pointed out an ad for auditions at a dinner theater, Glazer's life changed drastically.

His early days were spent in New York performing in the theater and taking odd jobs to make ends meet. Like many actors, he waited tables, drove a taxi, and even tried his hand at construction work — which fostered a love of carpentry he holds to this day. Glazer still performs on stage; recently he has appeared in *Staccato*, *Lunchtime*, *The Crucible*, and *Dylan* (in which he played poet Dylan Thomas).

In the early 1970s he moved to Los Angeles to seek work in film and television. His television debut was in an episode of *Quincy: M.D.*, but his first big role was on an episode of *Charlie's Angels*. Much to the delight of costars Peta Wilson and Don Francks, he told the story to interviewer Jane Hawtin when the three of them were interviewed: "It was my first costarring role on television and it was horrific. I mean for *me* it was yes, I was so — at that point — green that when it came time for my close-up, I would not move because I was afraid to get close to the camera. Not that I froze — the director gave me too many things to do: I had a huge cigar, I had a drink in my hand [and I] couldn't get it all out. Dick Gauthier, God bless him, said, 'Get rid of the cigar, the kid's got too much to do.'"

By the 1980s Glazer was appearing on the big screen alongside such artists as Liza Minnelli, Shelley Winters, Robert Townsend, Eddie Murphy, Keenan Ivory Wayans, Damon Wayans, John Hurt, Joe Pantoliano, and Ron Silver.

Glazer and his wife, actress Brioni Farrell, live in California. They have two grandchildren whom they visit often. When not in Toronto shooting *La Femme Nikita*, they visit family in Vancouver. Although Glazer enjoys gardening, carpentry, and cooking, his true passion is

researching the plight of prisoners of the Vietnam War still missing in action. His studies, which form the basis of a screenplay he is writing, have also figured strongly in his creation of Operations.

Filmography:

It's My Party, 1996; Scanner Cop II, 1995; Skyscraper, 1995; Bounty Tracker, 1993; Stepping Out, 1991; Eve of Destruction, 1991; Dollman, 1991; The Five Heartbeats, 1991; Nights, 1989; I'm Gonna Git You Sucka, 1988; Intruder, 1988; No Way Out, 1987; Hollywood Shuffle, 1987; Hunter's Blood, 1987; Vendetta, 1986; The Joy of Sex, 1984; Parts: The Clonus Horror, 1978

Television:

La Femme Nikita, 1997– ; While My Pretty One Sleeps (TVM), 1997; FX: The Series, 1996; Walker, Texas Ranger, 1994; The Substitute (TVM), 1993; Kung Fu: The Legend Continues, 1993; General Hospital, 1992; The Women of Windsor (TVM), 1992; E.N.G., 1993; Sweating Bullets, 1991–2 E.N.G., 1989; Twilight Zone, 1988; Whiz Kids, 1984; Charlie's Angels, 1980

Alberta Watson

Alberta Watson was born and raised in Toronto, Ontario, as Faith Susan Alberta Watson. Her mother, Grace, was a factory worker who struggled as a single mother to raise Susie, as she was known then, and her four half-siblings. When times got tough Alberta and one of her half-brothers stayed with Grace, and the rest of the kids went to live with their grandparents. Alberta never knew her father, Albert, who abandoned the family when she was still a baby.

Facing page: Eugene Robert Glazer signs posters at a fan convention.

Despite the financial hardships, Watson always felt loved and supported by her mother. At the age of 15, Watson dropped out of school and joined an alternative theater group called FOG, which operated out of the Bathurst Street United Church. There she caught the acting bug, and after a one-year stay on a commune-style farm in the country, she returned to Toronto to begin her career in earnest. She worked in commercials until she won a part in a CBC movie entitled *Honour Thy Father*, in which she was billed as Susan Watson. Unfortunately, her mother did not live to see her daughter's work and success. She died of Hodgkin's Disease when Alberta was only 19.

In her early twenties, Watson began to get noticed. In 1978, her performance as Mitzi in *In Praise of Older Women* garnered her a Genie nomination, and a year later her work in a short called *Exposure* won her the best actress award at the Yorkton Film Festival in Saskatchewan. Finally, in 1981, Watson got serious about getting some formal training and moved to New York to study with Gene Lasko.

For the next 10 years she made a living as a working actor, taking television and film roles and developing her craft before making the inevitable move to L.A. to pursue series work. Although she did work there, she didn't enjoy the "scene" and returned to New York in 1986 after just 18 months on the West Coast. Watson's career got a serious boost when she took the lead role in a small-budget independent film called *Spanking the Monkey*, in which she played a woman who begins a sexual relationship with her son. The film won the Sundance Film Festival's Audience Award, and Watson's performance was critically acclaimed.

She returned to Toronto and continued to work steadily, turning in marvelous performances in such films as *Shoemaker* and *The Sweet Hereafter*. In 1996, she won the role of Madeline, the master strategist, in *La Femme Nikita*. Working a very reasonable schedule of two to three days a week, she has been free to work in other projects, such as *The*

Facing page: Alberta Watson in her pre-Nikita days.

Girl Next Door opposite Henry Czerny. Watson lives in Toronto and spends as much free time as possible at her cottage near Haliburton, Ontario.

Filmography:

The Life Before This, 1999; *The Girl Next Door*, 1998; *The Sweet Hereafter*, 1997; *Bullet*, 1996; *Seeds of Doubt*, 1996; *Shoemaker*, 1996; *Sweet Angel Mine*, 1996; *Hackers*, 1995; *Spanking the Monkey*, 1994; *Zebrahead*, 1992; *The Hitman*, 1991; *Destiny to Order*, 1990; *White of the Eye*, 1987; *The Keep*, 1983; *The Soldier*, 1982; *Best Revenge*, 1982; *Black Mirror*, 1981; *Dirty Tricks*, 1980; *Stone Cold Dead*, 1979; *Exposure*, 1979; *In Praise of Older Women*, 1978; *Power Play*, 1978

Television:

La Femme Nikita, 1997– ; *Giant Mine* (TVM), 1996; *Gotti* (TVM), 1996; *A Child is Missing* (TVM), 1995; *The Outer Limits* (TVM), 1995; *Jonathan Stone: Threat of Innocence* (TVM), 1994; *Relentless: Mind of a Killer* (TVM), 1993; *Frame-Up* (TVM), 1993; *Law & Order*, 1990; *Island Son*, 1989; *Shannon's Deal* (TVM), 1989; *Red Earth, White Earth* (TVM), 1989; *Buck James*, 1987; *Fortune Dane*, 1986; *Women of Valor* (TVM), 1986; *The Equalizer*, 1985; *Kane & Abel* (miniseries), 1985; *Murder in Space* (TVM), 1985; *The Hitchhiker*, 1983; *Hill Street Blues*, 1981; *War Brides* (TVM), 1980; *King of Kensington*, 1975; *Honour Thy Father* (TVM), 1974

NIKITA COM: CONTACTING THE STARS OF THE SHOW

You can write to Roy Dupuis, Matthew Ferguson, Don Francks, Eugene Robert Glazer, Alberta Watson, Peta Wilson, or any of the cast or crew by addressing your letters to the following:

In Canada:

LFN Productions

565 Orwell St.

Mississauga, Ontario

L5A 2W4

In the United States:

USA Network

c/o Media Relations

1230 Avenue of Americas

New York, NY 10020-1513

By e-mailing at:

nikita@usanetwork.com

NIKITA.COM

CHARITIES

Better yet, consider showing your appreciation for their creativity by supporting one of their favorite charities.

Roy Dupuis:
The Mira Foundation
www.mira.ca
e-mail: miracan@cam.org

or write to:

Mira Foundation, attn: Christiane
1820 Rang Nord-Ouest
Sainte-Madeleine, Quebec, J0H 1S0
Canada
Tel: (450) 795-3725

Matthew Ferguson:
The Multiple Sclerosis Society of Canada
http://www.mssoc.ca/
e-mail: info@mssoc.ca

or write to:

Multiple Sclerosis Society of Canada
250 Bloor Street East, Suite 1000
Toronto, Ontario, M4W 3P9
Canada
Tel: (416) 922-6065
Fax: (416) 922-7538

Don Francks:

The Canada Tibet Committee

www.tibet.ca

e-mail: cantibet@tibet.ca

or write to:

The Canada Tibet Committee, National Office

4675 Coolbrook Avenue

Montreal, Quebec, H3X 2K7

Canada

Tel: (514) 487-0665

Fax: (514) 487-7825

Eugene Robert Glazer:

The Make-A-Wish Foundation of Canada

www.maw.org/

email: mawcan@istar.ca

or write to:

The Make-A-Wish Foundation of Canada

2208 Spruce Street

Vancouver, British Columbia, V6H 2P3

Canada

OR

Make-A-Wish Foundation of America

www.wish.org/

e-mail: mawfa@wish.org

NIKITA.COM

or write to:

Make-A-Wish Foundation Gift Center
P O Box 29119
Phoenix, AZ 85038
Tel: 1-800-757-5067

Alberta Watson :
The Toronto Wildlife Centre
60 John Drury Drive
Downsview, Ontario, M3K 2B8
Canada

Peta Wilson:
The Hospital for Sick Children
www.sickkids.on.ca/
e-mail: suzette.watson@sickkids.on.ca

or write to:

The Hospital for Sick Children Foundation
555 University Avenue
Toronto, Ontario, M5G 1X8
Canada
Tel: (416) 813-6166 or
1-800-661-1083

OR

Community Aid Abroad — Oxfam Australia
www.caa.org.au/index.html
e-mail: enquire@caa.org.au

or write to:

Community Aid Abroad — Oxfam Australia
156 George Street
Fitzroy Victoria 3065
Australia
Tel: +61 (0)3 9289 9444
Fax: +61 (0)3 9415 1879

NIKITA COM

INTERNET INTEL

There are hundreds of sites provided by and for fans with Internet access, and more are being added every week. There are clearly too many to review in detail. Provided here are summaries of the best and most popular *La Femme Nikita* sites, all of which provide links to other sites.

OFFICIAL SITES

Warner Brothers Site
http://www.lafemmenikita.com/

An entertaining and graphics-intensive site. This official site contains tons of information and multimedia treats including blooper clips featuring your favorite *La Femme Nikita* stars messing up, having fun, and playing jokes. The episode guide is disappointing, but the collection of unique official images and clips makes up for the site's shortcomings. The site also features a newsletter, chat site, and very active message board. Periodically, Warner Brothers promotes the show with contests for US citizens.

USA Network Site
http://www.usanetwork.com/series/nikita/

Again a minimal episode guide, containing only plot synopses with no cast or crew credits. This site contains a huge collection of high-quality official images, which fans can download and use on their own *La Femme Nikita* sites, and features bios of the cast members and an up-to-the-minute airing schedule.

FAN SITES

LJC's **La Femme Nikita Site**
http://ljc.simplenet.com/nikita/nikita.html

One of the best sites out there for *La Femme Nikita* fans, LJC's site has a strong emphasis on Peta Wilson. Well maintained and regularly updated, this site contains huge amounts of information culled from across the Web, and from "real world" sources. There are original exclusive offerings such as interviews with some of the creative talents that bring you the show. Possibly the most complete listing and archive of articles available. Highly recommended.

La Femme Nikita Anonymous
http://www.geocities.com/TelevisionCity/4163/

This is an excellent site, which includes enough information to keep any fan happy for hours and coming back for more. The site includes articles, pictures, and a great episode guide made up of plot summaries, spoilers, and images. A new section, "Wild Wacky Facts," is a great one-stop spot to pick up fun facts, many of which are summarized from Chris Heyn's posts to "Heyn's Hussies Message Board." Definitely check this one out.

Susan's La Femme Nikita . . . the Series
http://www.vci.net/~susanhar/lfn/

Great site with some unique features, including active work organizing charitable activities. Susan's site features some real multimedia treasures, including streamed video and audio appearances by *La Femme Nikita* cast members. Includes a cast favorite charity page — a great way to show your appreciation for what the actors do. New to the site,

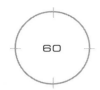

INTERNET INTEL

is the collection of script vs. aired transcripts, courtesy of Karen Hay. Simply wonderful.

Quinn's Page of La Femme Nikita and Roy Dupuis Images
http://quinn.simplenet.com/

Beautiful, well organized, and exhaustive, the site is filled with images, screen captures, and many unique pictures. The site features an excellent wallpaper section, as well. Make note of the user ID and password required to enter some sections of the site.

GC World
http://www.glasscurtain.com/

This site has gone through several incarnations, but remains a top *La Femme Nikita* fan site featuring fan fiction in The White Room. It also includes a good multimedia section.

Acceptable Collateral Acres — Row 8 Plot 30
http://www.row8plot30.com/lfn/

This is a unique site in terms of design and concept. You'll find some of the usual and the unusual presented in a highly original manner. Just to give you an idea of the site's sense of fun, there is a news section called the "Graveyard Grapevine" collected by "Catacomb Trolls"!

A La Vie — La Femme Nikita Site
http://alavie.tierranet.com/htmls/nikitamain.html

This is an extensive site with large collections of transcripts, articles, and images about *La Femme Nikita* and its stars. There are collages, wallpapers, and links to other collections on the Net, and a growing gallery of captured images from the episodes. The Dupuis "Observatory" is excellent. The site also includes a "bad boys" section with pictures of all the villains you love to hate.

The 1998 LFN Fan Website Awards
**http://geocities.com/TelevisionCity/Network/8450/
winners.html**

This spot is a great starting point to check out fan-voted favorite Web sites. See the best without spending hours searching.

Sounds of La Femme Nikita
http://member.aol.com/Cusmus/index.html

Simply the best single collection of information about the music used on *La Femme Nikita*. It includes links to record label sites — where you can often order those hard-to-find indie CDs — lyrics, and samples. Also includes band info and a music FAQ. Because of the work involved in maintaining this site, the content may not be as up-to-date as one might hope. Highly recommended nonetheless.

Cast and Character Sites

ROY DUPUIS
The Roy Dupuis Homepage
http://www.roydupuis.com/

An excellent site dedicated to actor Roy Dupuis, offered in French and English versions. There is an outstanding collection of information that includes a sizable image gallery, an extensive, illustrated filmography, biographical information, mailing list information, and membership information for the Roy Dupuis Fan Society.

Chloe's Roy Dupuis Homepage
http://www.iduna.demon.co.uk/roydupuis.htm

Excellent site. Chloe's Homepage contains the best collection of articles (most with pictures!) on Dupuis available online, as well as a small gallery of miscellaneous images. There are reviews, synopses, commentary, and images from most of the actor's stage, television, and theater work and helpful information on how to locate and purchase material available on video. The site also includes a message board for fans to chat and keep up on news about Dupuis, and an excellent links page.

Roy Dupuis Online Fan Site
http://members.xoom.com/_XOOM/roydupuis/main.html

This is a good-looking site with a *huge* gallery of pictures, some articles, and a few multimedia goodies.

Autodrome Granby
http://www.citenet.net/autodrome-granby/

This site advertises the events held at the Autodrome Granby stock-car racing track in Granby, Québec. Included is coverage of the June race held yearly to benefit Roy Dupuis's charity of choice, the Mira Foundation. The site offers information in French and English about the track and its events. On Friday, June 18, 1999, Dupuis acted as a pilot for a blind driver who competed in the Defi-Vision Race.

MATTHEW FERGUSON
Birkoff's Babes
http://www.geocities.com/TelevisionCity/Set/2695/

A fan site with some fun graphics, lots of images, several articles, and interviews with Matthew Ferguson and a message board for Birkoff fans.

DON FRANCKS

Walter's Wenches
http://www.geocities.com/TelevisionCity/Stage/2648/index.html

A fun fan page featuring the musings of a devoted band of Walter and Don Francks fans, for example, Walter's Wenches with code names like Frosted Tarts and Saucy Tarts. The site contains some great fan pictures of the actor, including one of his Model T Ford racing cars, and a few neat surprises courtesy of Mr. Francks himself.

EUGENE ROBERT GLAZER

The Official Eugene Robert Glazer Site
http://www.eugenerobertglazer.com/

A very good official fan-run site, which features news and updates on Glazer. Also contains a short biography, links, an interactive fan fiction link, a message board, Ops Quotes, and The Ultimate Operations Trivia Quiz.

ALBERTA WATSON

The Official Alberta Watson Site
http://www.albertawatson.com/

Excellent fan-run site with official status. Features all the news on Watson and an active message board occasionally visited by Alberta herself. You'll find an image gallery, a guide to the actress's work available on video, fan fiction, a monthly poll, and a trivia quiz.

RESOURCE LISTS

SectionZero
http://members.tripod.com/~Helix12/SZ/lfn.html

SectionZero contains an extensive links directory that will take you to the more obscure — and sometimes weird — *La Femme Nikita* sites.

CONVENTIONS & CHARITIES

Close Quarters Standby
http://www.logomancy.simplenet.com/SIDEKICKS/cqs.html

A fan-run convention since 1998 organized by the SideKicks Society (a group of fans of television's sidekicks!). Initially this group formed a group called Michael's Operatives (**http://logomancy.simple-net.com/SIDEKICKS/michael.html**) , which went on to take an interest in all things Nikita — and then some! In 1999 Convention Chair Robin Mayhall, along with Carol Burrell, Tara "LJC" O'Shea, and the rest of the Con Committee, were hard at work with the second annual convention to be held in Toronto in October. Visit the site for details about the conventions and information on past events (and read about the 1998 convention starting on page XX).

The Motion Picture Industry Charitable Alliance: Lights, Camera, Auction
http://www.mpica.org/LCA2/main.htm

Jon Cassar, Nigel Bennett, and John Kapelos founded this charitable organization, which auctions off television memorabilia to raise funds for noteworthy causes.

MESSAGE BOARDS

Besides the official message boards maintained at the official sites listed above, there are plenty of character-, cast-, and fan-driven sites out there. One site deserves a special mention for obvious reasons:

Heyn's Hussies
http://heynshussies.com/

A message board devoted to *La Femme Nikita* and featuring information provided by Chris Heyn, executive assistant to Joel Surnow. Great spot for inside information and spoilers.

MAILING LISTS

With dozens to choose from consider starting your search for a list that interests you by visiting:

http://www.onelist.com

NEWSGROUPS

alt.tv.lafemme-nikita
alt.fan.la-femme.nikita

CLOSE QUARTERS STANDBY:

The First La Femme Nikita Convention

On the weekend of October 2, 1998, fans held the first *La Femme Nikita* convention, affectionately titled "Close Quarters Standby." Nearly 300 faithful gathered at Toronto's Radisson Hotel Toronto East Don Valley for three days of fun, music, special guests, and a charity auction — which raised more than $17,000.

With three days of activities it is impossible to do the entire event justice. For fan diaries and more personal descriptions of the weekend check out the many *La Femme Nikita* Web sites, or do a Web search for "Close Quarters Standby." You won't be disappointed! The convention organizers have constructed an informative site to keep fans up to date on future and past events:

http://logomancy.simplenet.com/SIDEKICKS/cqs.html.

Saturday's highlight was an array of special guests, who graciously accepted invitations to speak and meet with fans. It was an exciting privilege to hear from some of the creative people who devote so much of their energy to making the show the best it can be. The artists and storytellers shared their unique insights into how much of a cooperative effort each hour is. The afternoon included a screening of the blooper reel and ended with an autograph session. What follows is not a verbatim transcript of what the panelists told us that day, or of the question and answer periods, but a reconstruction of the more interesting things we learned.

The guests, in order of appearance, were: Chris Heyn (assistant to Joel Surnow) and Natalie Folkes (script supervisor); David Thompson (editor); Rocco Matteo (set designer, in a videotaped tour of the studio); Jim and Geoff Murrin (prop designers); Laurie Drew (costume designer); and Don Francks and Matthew Ferguson ("Walter" and "Birkoff").

Chris Heyn
And Natalie Folkes

Chris Heyn and Natalie Folkes were funny and forthcoming and gave us all a peek inside the production side of La Femme Nikita.

Joel Surnow is the executive consultant and the creator of La Femme Nikita's style, both visually and in terms of the music. The show has several in-house writers (Michael Loceff, Robert Cochran, Peter Lenkov [joining the staff], and David Irwin [just departing]). Apparently, York Peppermint Patties play a large role in keeping sugar levels up for the writing staff! The story-writing process was discussed in some detail. First, the staff get together and hash out story ideas, and these may be farmed out to freelance writers or kept in-house. They do get spec scripts sent via agents, including scripts from women writers. But for the most part, Heyn says, they have a problem finding writers who "get" the show.

Scripts pass through several stages (first draft outline, second draft outline, first draft teleplay, second draft teleplay) and then Michael Loceff will put a final polish on the script if need be.

One of the most popular questions they get asked is how to break into the writing business. The producers get a lot of submissions by freelance writers but what they prefer to read is a script for another

Natalie Folkes and Chris Heyn at Close Quarters Standby, 1998.

television show (like NYPD Blue or Law and Order, for instance). From such a script they can get an idea of how well the person writes. Their advice for aspiring writers? Read scripts — lots of them — and books about writing. Show business is about relationships and contacts, so don't be shy. He added that it is a good idea to have an agent, but agents may not be as effective as you might think. Mr. Heyn was emphatic on one point: the La Femme Nikita staff does not accept unsolicited scripts. All unsolicited scripts and ideas are sent back unread; he added that fan fiction was a good forum for such creative endeavors.

When the script is complete, Chris Heyn uses MovieMaster (a computer program) to format the script appropriately, and he then e-mails it to Natalie Folkes. She submits it to producer Jamie Paul Rock, and on his approval the script is sent along to the "production keys" (Rocco Matteo, Laurie Drew, and so on). Discussions then take place about the story. Is it possible to reproduce the location or setting in Toronto? Will the budget support a scene with a twenty-man assault team or will the scene have to be rewritten for a five-man team? These are the practical and logistical questions that get answered before the script begins a stage called preparation. Jamie Paul Rock plays a huge role in the production. His great strength is that he thinks in terms of the story. He juggles budget and location considerations so that they best serve the story.

The standard schedule is seven days of preparation followed by seven days of shooting. The episode then goes to post-production for special effects and editing work. Preparation begins with a concept meeting after everyone has seen the script. The big question is: can the show be done? The department heads are asked for their input, the prop department may bring in samples, and Joel Surnow participates in all of it. If necessary, the script goes back to the writers for revisions. Ms. Folkes attends all of these meetings and she also meets with the assistant directors to be sure the sequences for the second unit will work (these are the action sequences where the stunt people do most of their work). There is some flexibility but the bottom line is cost and whether it can be done. Ms. Folkes stays in contact with the L.A. office until the script has final approval; she is usually juggling three to four scripts in different stages of readiness at any one time. Sometimes discovering a new location can drive a rewrite, and occasionally a sequence will be reshot if the idea doesn't work on film.

One of Chris Heyn's other tasks is to download fan comments from the message boards on the Web. Both positive and negative comments are printed for the staff to peruse. Surnow reads them regularly, and Michael Loceff apparently loves to read them as soon as they are available. Heyn often hears him laughing in his office as he reads some of the funnier submissions.

Chris Heyn also oversees the content of the official Web site and monitors the submissions to the message board. Frequently Mr. Heyn will answer fans' questions and submit an inside scoop on a current shoot or future guest star or even tease fans with hints about future plotlines. To further this end fans set up a Web site where you can post questions and read past discussions. *Heyn's Hussies* is located at: **http://www.heynshussies.com/**

Nikita storyboard artist K. Douglas MacRae at Close Quarters Standby 1999.

The mike was opened up for questions from the floor. Someone asked if HAL from 2001: *A Space Odyssey* was the inspiration for Brutus in "Last Night." HAL was referred to during production but the writers and designers wanted to make Brutus unique. Writers pull inspiration and references from the world around them, and look for the feel of an inspiring film or literary work. They obviously don't seek to reproduce the source of their inspiration. Robert Cochran, for example, has been inspired by such sci-fi favorites as *Foundation* and *Dune*.

Occasionally, one fan commented, it is obvious that stand-ins are being used. Michael's stand-in, Brian, watches tapes and studies Michael's walk and movements and will double for Dupuis from time to time when there are shooting time restrictions.

"Not Was," a second-season fan favorite, was written with Internet fans in mind. But Chris Heyn said there is a large male audience and a large viewing audience that is not represented on the Net, and the producers are very aware of this. Although the feedback over the Web is convenient for some fans, many viewers don't have access, and the show receives a great deal of its fan response through written letters. These letters do represent a different demographic group than the Net postings, and the show's staff keeps this in mind.

There were some comments from the floor bemoaning the lack of women writers on the show and the loss of a female voice in the writing. Naomi Janzen did some writing in the first season, but since then the episodes have been written by an entirely male staff. Efforts are made to find good female writers but the panelists emphasized that finding good writers who could write well for the show (regardless of sex) was an extremely difficult task. At this point in the series the characters are so well established and well known by the writing staff that it is not a problem to write for them. The actors compensate and make up the difference by bringing the female point of view to the process.

Other insights included that the Jurgen story arc was originally proposed as a six-episode arc, and the character's death was envisioned right from the start. The gray areas and ambivalent aspects of the series are *La Femme Nikita*'s great strengths, and the Jurgen story played to those strengths. The 90 degree and 180 degree turns of the stories and the characters really engage the fans.

"Section-speak" has been the brainchild of Michael Loceff, primarily. Loceff teaches math and computer science at a college in Northern California and has a love of words. He researches and explores new words to add to the Section vocabulary and loves to create new words. He has concocted at least four of the terms himself.

In short, Heyn and Folkes summed up the past two years' efforts by saying that the strength of Season One lay in its individual episodes, the second season had a strong overall arc, and Season Three would be a good blend of these two strengths.

David Thompson

The next guest of the afternoon was David Thompson, who shares editing duties with two other editors, Richard Wells and Robert K. Sprogis (and earlier with Eric Goddard). Thompson assumes the lion's share of the assignments, editing 22 of the 44 episodes that comprised Seasons One and Two (he edits every other show).

David Thompson at Close Quarters Standby '98.

Initially Thompson professed a nervousness at having to address a roomful of people, claiming that he chose a career where he sits in a dark room to avoid such traumas! He was funny, informative, and extremely generous when it came to answering all our detailed questions.

Introduced as the artist behind the universally admired opening sequence to "Rescue," he didn't have to wait long before he was asked about the scene. There are only six shots of Michael and Nikita (that is, Roy and Peta) in the opening sequence; all the action is done with doubles and stunt people. It's the work done by the second unit that provides the footage to make a sequence like this one work. The scene took two days to shoot and three days to edit. There were three hours of footage for the opening sequence and seven hours for the rest of the episode.

Thompson uses an AVID (film composer) editing machine. When he begins to edit he has seven days of material to work with. The footage is loaded into the computer daily, and as the footage arrives he does non-linear cutting. The script provides a loose structure for what is done; the footage is the raw material. It takes seven to eight days to edit an episode.

The music is in place by the start of the shoot, and he works to marry the beats of the scene with the piece of music. Some bands don't mind their pieces being manipulated somewhat, while others will only allow fades in and out. In rare cases he works with an entire piece of music and will work the scene to fit the music. This was the case with the opening scene of the "Rescue" episode. In addition to using the beautiful composition by Enigma, "Beyond the Invisible" (his favorite), it was Thompson who requested that they not lay in the sound of gunfire. The result was simply brilliant.

The style of the show gives the editor great liberty. A lot of close-ups are used, but not a lot of wide shots. Thompson described this as the "Russian style of editing." For the most part, the editor has a free hand with the episode and then the director has two to three days to rework it.

The editor rarely visits the set — maybe once or twice a year — but he does spend two to three days a week in L.A. where he sits with Joel Surnow to discuss what is and is not working with an episode. If a scene doesn't work Surnow will throw it out and reshoot to make it work. If dialogue needs to be cut it can be done in post-production and, again, that decision lies with the producer. Once back in Toronto, Thompson will have three days of dailies waiting for him to start work on. He puts in a 60-hour work week and is free to set his own schedule, adding that he loves his work so much he would edit for free!

The show is shot on Super16 and converted to 3/4 inch digital beta by the assistant editor. The PC holds four to five episodes. The episode is edited and the cut is sent in VHS format by courier to Surnow in L.A. The team considered a direct-line feed but found it was too expensive. Thompson feels the personal touch is needed anyway; he has to be in the room with Surnow. He emphasized, smiling, that it was no chore to fly down to California.

Don Francks playfully bows to his co-stars, Alberta Watson and Eugene Robert Glazer at Close Quarters Standby '99.

He acknowledged the influence of the so-called MTV style (quick edits cut to music) but emphasized that it is Joel Surnow who provides the direction for the style of the show. One criticism of the Canadian style is that it can be too slow and, while the American style is faster, Surnow wants a European look and feel for the series. He said he loves that the show takes chances and enjoys that the style allows him to linger on faces.

Some miscellaneous notes:
- When asked about the use (the questioner felt overuse) of the shaky-cam and tilty-cam effects, Thompson confessed he was glad the directors don't employ it as often anymore. He has had to edit 17 hours straight of tilty-cam footage (the director liked the *Batman* movie that employed that style of camera work).
- The choice to keep Michael's butt scene was Joel Surnow's.
- Director T.J. Scott brought a new style to the show, one he used to shoot for *Top Cops*.

- Thompson really loves the footage from the "Rescue" explosion and he did use it for "Mercy" but he does try not to get caught doing that. As he cuts, he'll intercut scenes to keep up audience interest (and his own) in the action.

Thompson was asked whether he's had to cut around anyone's performances. He was emphatic that there was no one he had to cut around, pointing to the actors' good work. He said he enjoyed working with Peta Wilson's work but confessed that Don Francks is his personal favorite. He does lose scenes or cuts that he likes from time to time and particularly hates losing a Walter scene. Joel Surnow is sometimes forced to cut because of time constraints and although Thompson won't fight with a director or producer, he will use his powers of persuasion to save a cut if he thinks it's warranted. He wins about half the time.

Rocco Matteo

In a 45-minute video tour, production designer Rocco Matteo guided us through the labyrinth of the *La Femme Nikita* studios. The studio of 35,000 square feet includes space to house the four department heads in offices that take up about one eighth of the total space.

Matteo discussed aspects of Nikita's apartment, such as its openness and its modernity. The idea is to give Nikita a calm place away from Section. Unlike her time in Section, where she has to be guarded and self-protective, here she can be emotionally open, her moods and thoughts more visible. The walls slide out of the way to make room for camera equipment, affording the directors the opportunity to shoot the character and the space from many angles.

Early on Peta brought things of her own to the set to personalize the space, but as the first season wore on and the second season began there was less and less of Peta present in the decoration. (Even Nikita seems less present as her space becomes more modern and pared down.) Similarly, Operations has his area from which he overlooks everyone and everything, but it's still a question whether or not he has his own environment as such.

The *La Femme Nikita* studio in Mississauga, Ontario.

The designers have established both visual and dramatic depths by creating separate lairs within the central operations area. Camera movement between the areas is important to the production, not just in practical terms but also in terms of storytelling and character exploration. The various tiers of space, for example, reflect the power structure and elements of character and identity. At this time Walter's domain is small, and Matteo said he was looking to expand it — which, of course, he did with new storage and security functions, a back room, and a rear mezzanine.

The White Room acts as the central icon of Section. It's a small space, tall, cylindrical, and consequently without corners. The space is both intimate and adversarial. In television production it is traditional to avoid the use of white. But the *Nikita* designers deliberately broke with this, embracing the cold, shadowless, depthless look.

The Gambit Room is the twin of the White Room with some variations. It has an observation gallery so characters can be both part of and removed from an interrogation at the same time. The booth also allows observers to be sonically or visually removed (observing from behind a darkened window).

Designers reuse strong geometric forms over and over again to create visual rhythms and points of reference. New environments are

Alberta Watson at the 1999 convention.

planned and have already been added. Systems is a new space for the second season. The use of vertical space will also be expanded. We've seen this in "Adrian's Garden" particularly, and earlier in some of the ant-farm style shots of the catwalks.

Madeline's office has undergone a significant change. The old office still exists in Section, according to Matteo, but the character has new interests, such as her cultivation of plants. Birkoff has some personal stuff in his area but generally the rule of thumb is no clutter. Clutter distracts the eye, and the idea here is to focus on an individual's strengths. Gone are the cookies and sweets of the early episodes; even the joystick is rarely seen.

Matteo encourages the writers to expand and extend the voyage of being in Section. If they write it and it's within budget Matteo will build it. It takes about three to four weeks to prepare an environment for filming, which not only means building it, but wiring it for lights, monitors, and gadgets.

Jim and Geoff Murrin

Before Laurie Drew was introduced all hell broke loose with a little skit "Section's been breached!" someone yelled. To the rescue and quite unexpectedly, out popped the "Goatee twins" Jim and Geoff Murrin. What a blast! The room went nuts with everyone up out of their chairs to welcome the pair and catch a glimpse of the hijinks at the front of the room. When things settled down the twins sat down to chat with us and answer some audience questions.

The Murrin brothers aren't just another pair of pretty faces — well, one face, I guess, on two persons! These two do the props for the show. They have been making props for 10 or 11 years and have worked on such Canadian television shows as *Top Cops*, *Nancy Drew*, *The Hardy Boys*, and the feature film *Highway 61*.

One of the brothers made his *La Femme Nikita* debut as a drunk on the ground next to his dog. But don't look for it on your tapes of the show; the scene was cut from the Season One episode. But he did appear in the Hong Kong scene to fill out the crowd. When Joel Surnow was looking to cast someone for the second-season teaser for the conspiracy, director Jon Cassar suggested Jim and Geoff. Surnow asked them if they could handle some lines, and they jumped at the chance: "Yes, please!" The conspiracy ploy was so successful and popular with fans that the twins joked they could work the gig into a spin-off series!

Here are some of the answers generated by audience questions: Props for the show are designed from scratch. Sometimes they will

"Goatee Men" Jim and Geoff Murrin at Close Quarters Standby '98.

source out the work or make a hybrid item by bringing together bits and pieces of different objects to create something entirely new. Generally, La Femme Nikita does not offer extreme challenges for the props department. The so-called "sneaker ball bomb" (used by Michael in "Love") was one item that was discussed. Jam is a local design house that does props, and they did various versions of the bomb. One model was designed to sit still and blow up, and the others were designed to roll through the air ducts. This house also builds props for Earth: Final Conflict.

The brothers Murrin stuck around for the rest of the afternoon and joined Matthew Ferguson and Don Francks for the autograph session. There were no pictures of them to sign, but they remained undeterred, drawing cartoon versions of themselves on the stills featuring other characters, complete with little dialogue balloons mocking themselves or other characters. They were very generous with their time and their spirits and much appreciated by the audience.

Laurie Drew

Laurie Drew's presence was a real treat. The Gemini Awards had been held the previous evening, and Ms. Drew had been up all night celebrating her win for Best Costume (for "Noise"). She looked great, beautifully accessorized with her award! She was particularly pleased to receive the award because it is so rare for a designer to win for contemporary costume; designers of period costume traditionally garner awards in this category.

She spoke of the actors in the show, saying it was wonderful to work with all of them. Of the two leads in the show she said that Peta Wilson has great energy and integrity. She's a beautiful woman whose experience as a runway model only helps when it comes to carrying off the clothes they purchase or design and sew (build) for the character. Roy Dupuis is easier to design for, as Michael wears one suit. She was joking, of course, but the variety of Michael's attire is considerably narrower than Nikita's. Dupuis is not particularly fond of

Laurie Drew shows off some of the costumes she has designed for La Femme Nikita.

fittings and usually has two for the season. He is no problem to build for, though, as he has a perfect ten-inch drop. Before you get any ideas about what *that* means, the term describes the ten-inch difference between his chest measurement and his waist measurement, of 42 and 32 inches respectively.

The process of costume design is a collaborative one. Ms. Drew elaborated: when she reads the script, costumes come into her mind right away, and she discusses her ideas with the producer. The directors often bring ideas, as well, making it a genuine team process. The script is read and the budget is broken down with the department heads so they know what kind of money they have to work with. Location also plays a factor in costume design decisions: Drew and her team examine numerous photographs, looking for the context of the location, and the demands of action on the character, and deciding who else might be in the scene. If they don't buy the clothing, they build it in-house. They start with a sketch, look at swatches, buy the material and can have a piece ready by the following day.

She says the designers don't really design for themselves because they don't have the time. Drew wears whatever is most comfortable (and warm for the winter shoots). Her day starts early: she's up at 5 a.m. in order to be on the set and usually gets home at about 9 or 10 p.m. Consequently, she never thinks about looking good while she's working. The Gemini ceremonies were a chance to get dressed up for a night.

It takes about seven days to do each show, so at that pace a good deal happens by virtue of accident (both good and bad). A typical week will require about five hundred decisions on Laurie Drew's part, and the team will juggle three episodes in various stages of readiness: one will be prepping, one shooting, and one wrapping. She praised her crew unreservedly, saying they "save my butt day in and day out." They round up resources, build outfits, and are on the shoot handling the demands there.

When asked what influence the actors might have on costume decisions, Drew replied that there was indeed a personal relationship between the actors and the clothes. The chemistry of the actors when

Laurie Drew at the Gemini Awards with her award for costume design in "Noise."

she first meets them — their body, their vibe, their power, and their sexuality — all influence a designer. Essentially, what may look good on the rack won't necessarily look good on the person. And Peta Wilson, in particular, exerts a very strong influence and involvement over costume choices. The actress is very busy as she is in almost every scene, so Drew puts together a rack of items for Wilson to look at. It may be several hours before she has a few free minutes, and when she does they look through the selections together quickly. Wilson will try on some of the outfits. Often she'll choose an outfit for a scene because she knows the scene very well and has definite ideas about what will work.

Nobody donates clothing just to have it seen on the show. The retailers and designers are in business to make money, but many offer special service considerations, such as free fittings and a "pay for what you keep" arrangement when shipping clothing to the studio. Ms. Drew emphasized that show business is a *business*, and she sees no reason it should be catered to or offered special privileges.

The show does buy from outside design houses, and Peta Wilson is very supportive of local talent. For example, the backless dress of the Season Two finale was created by Toronto designer Crystal Seimans. And Drew and her team designed and built the red dress used in the art gallery scene in "Noise." She's very proud of the garment, and brought it for fans to see, along with the long shirt-coat and several other items. The dress is cut on the bias and consequently can fit a range of sizes from two to six. Not surprisingly, Nikita's wardrobe is the largest and Michael's is the smallest.

When asked if we would see Michael wearing something other than his dark suit, Ms. Drew replied that it is unlikely, except when Michael is undercover. The character as written is nearly two-dimensional and his wardrobe is practical and functional; in other words, his economy of movement and emotion is matched by an economy of dress. She joked that she imagined the character had twenty of the same suit in his closet. His jacket is 100% fine light wool from Paris. Roy Dupuis dresses completely differently from his alter ego. In real life he uses a lot of color.

Don Francks brought in his own bandanas and insisted that his character wear them. Much of Walter's wardrobe is drawn directly from the actor's style. For Birkoff, Drew uses softer textures and lines that suggest an urban street look.

As the characters evolve and take on a life of their own the designer has to keep up with these changes to prevent the looks becoming dated or flat. Nikita started out hustling on the street (tough and strong), and over the course of her training she acquired refinement and style. The character's conflicts are reflected in her costume. She started out rough and raw, fighting Section all the way, but now she tries not to show as much of her inner life and motivations, guarding herself to prevent Section from using any revelations against her. Still, there is a continuity to the design and costume, which Drew maintains.

When asked if the costumes ever get destroyed on the set, she said it does happen. Peta Wilson is a very physical person, as is her character, so occasionally, heels will snap, but she said Wilson is respectful of the clothing, and damage is rare. This prompted a question about the shoes she chooses for Nikita. Drew lamented the current trend toward big clunky shoes, stating that the only really nice ones out there right now are very expensive (more than $500). She favors high heels with long toes for Nikita's elegant looks and talked about the new spy boot she was developing for Nikita's third-season look.

She was asked if she had any tips for the fashion-impaired. After the laughter settled down, she said if she had one single tip to offer it was buy vintage clothing. The quality of the older garments surpasses that of today's fashions. There are a lot of really bad clothes out there (and a few good expensive ones), but nowadays it can even be hard to find really good fabric. If you can afford it, seamstresses and tailors can create good garments, but for those who can't afford it, vintage clothing provides good design and good fabric at a more reasonable price. Ditto for shoes. The expensive shoes used on the show are out of most people's reach, but for quality and style, she says, again look for vintage items.

Matthew Ferguson and Don Francks

The room went nuts when the special guests of honor finally appeared. Don Francks and Matthew Ferguson came out together and stayed for an autograph session. They talked for a while and took questions from the floor as the informal chat meandered from topic to topic.

Ferguson auditioned in Toronto. He had been called back for a Canadian miniseries called *Peacekeepers* but didn't get the part, despite having auditioned four times. In the end, he was told he didn't have the look they were going for (his hair was long at the time). Aggravated, he got his neighbor, Alice, to give him a buzz cut. A week later he was called in to audition for *La Femme Nikita* for the part of Hacker. The rest, as they say is history.

Don Francks originally auditioned for the part of Operations, but the casting people thought he'd be great for Walter, whom Francks refers to affectionately as a "warm, old freak." He also told us proudly that Walter's signature nickname for Nikita, "Sugar," was not in the script and was his invention. Fans will also recognize that deep throaty purr of Walter's as another Francks trademark!

Ferguson and Francks have a good rapport and spend a lot of their downtime together talking about music. Francks has been working on a CD, which he laughingly calls "The Desperation I Can Handle, It's the Hope That's Killing Me." Fans wanted to know how like their characters the two actors are. Ferguson said that he wasn't a computer nerd and that it was only through Birkoff that he was becoming computer literate.

Matthew Ferguson and Don Francks entertain the crowd at the '98 convention.

Asked whether he'd been working with his daughter, Cree Summer, Francks lit up like the proud father he so clearly is. He said they had worked together on the animated series *Inspector Gadget* and that his daughter had been singing with him and his band from the time she was nine years old. Lenny Kravitz produced her album *Street Faerie* for Sony.

Besides an active career in music, Francks has a passion for collecting cars. He collects Harley-Davidson motorcycles and has a collection of Model T Ford racing cars, the oldest 1927. He takes them apart and fixes them. He also has an interest in airships, in spite of his wife's protests that "they're phallic." He was also most proud of his marriage and its longevity: he and his wife have been married for 31 years.

Both actors look forward to their scenes together, and that shows onscreen. Ferguson added that it was always more fun to play with a live actor rather than a blank computer screen, and loved the fact that

Matthew Ferguson

Birkoff had a girlfriend, enabling him to act with Tara Slone. Ferguson theorized that Birkoff was in Section because he probably hacked into some computer he shouldn't have.

They talked a bit about their co-workers. Roy Dupuis is "a lot of fun." He teaches Ferguson about computers, and they practise French together. Dupuis is a complete sound addict, a real audio-phile. Francks teased that "his whole house is a speaker" and that he can tell you each make and model number of every component in the place. He has a great sense of humor but can be a loner sometimes. Gene (Eugene Robert Glazer) is also close, and spends much of his down-time with them, making them something of a trio. They spoke of his interest in the Vietnam War and his desire to make a film about the subject. Unlike his onscreen character, he is a very funny man.

In fact, the whole cast shares a tremendous sense of humor. Glazer has been in the business for some time and tells great stories. Alberta Watson, Ferguson said, has a big heart and he admires her art greatly, saying he learns about acting every day just watching the choices she makes. She's subtle and clear. Francks talked about Peta Wilson, saying that she is going all the time and you can't keep her down. He said just the physical demands of her schedule alone are grueling and that she is one of the hardest-working women in television.

Ferguson was asked how old he was, to which he answered, "Birkoff is 21." After much laughter and coyness he said he just asks the casting agent, "How old do you want me to be?" He described Claude Watson, the performing-arts school at which he trained, saying it was a great school. They had guest artists in every week, he was educated in voice and movement. In short, they taught him what it is to be an actor. He was also asked if he had any input into Birkoff's costume, to which he replied that one of the strongest elements on the show was the look, and Laurie Drew is largely responsible for that. He trusted her direction in these matters and said he only once turned down a costume choice.

The Murrin brothers asked the final question: In a battle between Walter and Operations, who would win? Francks replied with his usual twinkle that Operations would win, "Cause Walter loves to make love, not war!"

LA FEMME NIKITA
EPISODE GUIDE

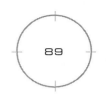

Season One		Season Two		Season Three	
101	Nikita	201	Hard Landing	301	Looking for Michael
102	Charity	202	Spec Ops	302	Someone Else's Shadow
103	Love	203	Third Person	303	Opening Night Jitters
104	Simone	204	Approaching Zero	304	Gates of Hell
105	Friend	205	New Regime	305	Imitation of Death
106	Treason	206	Mandatory Refusal	306	Love and Country
107	Mother	207	Darkness Visible	307	Cat and Mouse
108	Escape	208	Half Life	308	Outside the Box
109	Gray	209	First Mission	309	Slipping into Darkness
110	Choice	210	Open Heart	310	Under the Influence
111	Rescue	211	Psychic Pilgrim	311	Walk On By
112	Innocent	212	Soul Sacrifice	312	Threshold of Pain
113	Gambit	213	Fuzzy Logic	313	Beyond the Pale
114	Recruit	214	Old Habits	314	Hand to Hand
115	Obsessed	215	Inside Out	315	Before I Sleep
116	Missing	216	Not Was	316	I Remember Paris
117	Noise	217	Double Date	317	All Good Things
118	Voices	218	Off Profile	318	Third Party Ripoff
119	War	219	Last Night	319	Any Means Necessary
120	Verdict	220	In Between	320	Three-Eyed Turtle
121	Brainwashed	221	Adrian's Garden	321	Playing With Fire (Part I)
122	Mercy	222	End Game	322	On Borrowed Time (Part II)

(Please note that the episode numbers refer to the airing order and are not the production numbers.)

SEASON ONE

101 NIKITA

Written by Cyrus Nowrasteh
Directed by Jon Cassar

Nikita, a street kid, stumbles across a murder in progress in a back alley and is discovered holding the murder weapon she has wrested from the killer. Imprisoned for a crime she did not commit, she awakens in Section One (a secret antiterrorist organization), is told she is dead to the world, and is trained to become an assassin.

The first episode, "Nikita," wastes no time establishing the tone and major themes of the series. The opening sequence intercuts scenes of street-kid Nikita (Nikita struts, mouths off, runs with her pals, eats pizza, panhandles, plays with a kitten in a rainy alley) with shots of her strapped to a table in a white room. Visually the sequence is arresting; the contrast between the grime of the urban streets and the sterile and overlit white room is stark in the extreme. The kitten scene is a little too cute, but it establishes Nikita's soft spot for the helpless, echoes her life as an alleycat and is redeemed in the next episode, where we see she has a pet cat.

Nikita is a survivor, trapped by circumstances first on the street (after her mother kicks her out of the house), then in prison (mistakenly jailed for the murder of a police officer), and finally in Section One (having been unwillingly "recruited"). In faking her death in prison, Section has turned her into a nonperson and stripped her of any hope of clearing her name in the civilian world.

Thus Nikita joins the ranks of such classic TV heroes as Patrick McGoohan's *The Prisoner*, David Janssen's *The Fugitive*, and Bruce Greenwood's *Nowhere Man*, who fight to preserve their identities. Nikita's innocence is the series' principal point of departure from Luc

L — corner of Yonge and Dundas Streets, looking north
S — Nikita hangs out on the streets at the beginning of the episode

Besson's original film. Series producer Joel Surnow and actress Peta Wilson agreed that reinventing Nikita as the innocent victim of circumstance would give the audience its point of identification. It would also serve to create the central source of dramatic conflict in the character's drive to retain her humanity — and simply survive — in the face of such a loss of freedom, control, and identity.

Stylistically, the show begins by breaking one of the first rules of television production design. White is a color that is never used, and its stark unfamiliarity is employed to great effect here. In later episodes the "White Room" will become identified with Madeline's ruthless interrogation techniques. The room is like a tiled, cold, windowless well with no corners and nowhere to hide; the occupant is observed, monitored, and fully exposed. This voyeurism is pervasive throughout Section. By contrast, the white hospital room exploits notions of exposure and vulnerability and becomes the scene of several truthful exchanges.

"Nikita" also features a signature element of the series: the music.

*All location photos in the episode guide were taken in Toronto, Canada. Below each photo is a description of the physical location (L) of the shot, and the scene (S) in which the location is used in the show.

EPISODE GUIDE

Here the music of indie band Thrive creates a stylish and unfamiliar backdrop for the action, with soft dreamy vocals holding their own against harsh instrumentation. This juxtaposition finds its way into many of music supervisor Blaine Johnson's choices for musical additions, nicely complementing Sean Callery's evocative original scores. Female vocalists abound, often acting as Nikita's "voice" or underlining action or the emotional content of a scene. Johnson's selections are frequently unknown or little-known pieces by mainly small or independent bands. The music is a most important contribution to the style and feel of the series, and the fact that for most of the audience the pieces are unrecognizable creates the feeling that these pieces were written specifically for the show. The choice to forgo the use of enormously popular tunes helps to reinforce the otherness of *La Femme Nikita*, as does the international flavor of the cast, locations, and the five-minutes-into-the-future gadgets and fashions.

Music

"The Theme to *La Femme Nikita*" by **Mark Snow** on *La Femme Nikita: Music from the Television Series* (TVT Records) — opening theme

"Revenge" by **Thrive** on *Thrive* (Spider Records) — the teaser crime scene

"Big Mistake" by **Chainsuck** on *Angel Score* (TVT Records) — Nikita's training

"3 AM" by **Tristan Psionic** on *TPA Flight 028* (Sonic Unyon) — ambush at ambulance

"All To Myself" by **Philosopher Kings** on *Philosopher Kings* (Sony Music Canada) — Nikita decorates her apartment

"Blood Red" by **Rose Chronicles** on *Happily Ever After* (Nettwerk) — Nikita burns picture of her grave

Guest Cast

Bill MacDonald (Van Vactor), Anais Granofsky (Carla), Ric Reid (Stan), Robbie Rox (Stokes)

102 CHARITY

Written by Robert Cochran
Directed by Kari Skogland

In "Charity" we are treated to Nikita's first "Valentine Mission," in which she is required to romance a criminal named Alec Chandler. Nikita starts to fall for the charismatic benefactor of a local shelter for homeless street youth, unaware that he is using these shelters as a cover for a global slave trade.

"Charity" takes a hackneyed, predictable story line and gives it its own Nikita twist. Unfortunately, there are several unworthy moments. Nikita's "roll and rescue" is not enough to cover a gratuitous peek up Nikita's skirts. Peta Wilson has one of her self-described "hit the mark and bark" moments during her confrontation with Chandler, but the writer has left her with little choice: "You sell children. You're scum!" *Yikes.* Earlier, during Skyler's interrogation, the actress is struggling to pin down her character, yet she is able to evoke Nikita's inexperience by drawing on some of her own.

We can now add little children to lost kittens on Nikita's list of attractions. However, director Kari Skogland rescues a potentially saccharine moment with some unusual camerawork and dreamlike music that makes us believe we are getting a glimpse of Nikita on a mental holiday from Section. Arguably, it is this unguarded moment that catches Chandler's attention more than Section's cutesy setup.

Humorous moments include a sugared-out Birkoff killing time with a joystick and computer game. Nikita's verbal sparring with Birkoff also hints at the "little brother-big sister" relationship they will develop. And Madeline's instruction to Michael about the red evening jacket is a sly wink to the audience about Michael's signature monochromatic look. Dupuis gets playful as Michael plays at drunkenness aboard Chandler's yacht.

Nikita and Walter begin the first in a long series of flirtations.

L — The Esplanade and Scott
  Street
S — The "balloon scene"; Nikita
  first meets Chandler

Above:
L — The Captain Matthew Flinders, docked at
  Harbourfront
S — Chandler's boat
Left:
L — Queens Quay subway terminal;
  Harbourfront
S — Nikita loses Chandler's man

Beyond the sexual innuendo and teasing, the strength of the Nikita-Walter connection is its humanity. Walter repeatedly serves as a touchstone for Nikita and a caring voice within Section. In a business populated by young people in physically demanding jobs with a reduced life expectancy, Walter is a rarity: older, wiser, and more humane than most. How has he done it, how has he survived, and why is he there?

Notable is the rare (take a picture 'cause it'll last longer) smile from Michael occasioned by Nikita's confidence in her own ability to interest Chandler. Presumably, the potential for a connection between the two agents has not gone unnoticed over the course of Nikita's training. Several moments in this episode suggest that the mission is as much a test for Michael as it is for Nikita: the scene in Madeline's office, Operation's comment on Nikita's growing affection for Chandler, Michael's impatience and discomfort while he eavesdrops during Nikita and Chandler's dance, his appearance in Nikita's apartment, waiting like a jealous lover. That the relationship is and will be more problematic than office politics can explain away is firmly established in the final act. Nikita pulls a gun on Michael, and his submission — the kiss on her hand and the suggestive stroking of the gun's barrel — defines the fascinating and dysfunctional central relationship of the series. The connections between violence and sex, self-hatred and manipulation finally find expression in near sado-masochism by Season Two's opening story arc. Dupuis and Wilson create electricity between their characters. Wilson gives the scene even more power as Nikita smells and tastes the skin Michael has just touched (a gesture that is reprised at the close of "Hard Landing").

Section is hoist by its own petard, so to speak. Nikita, we are learning, is humane in her impulses and motivations. She acts independently to right perceived wrongs. Operations keeps her in the dark so that she'll "operate more effectively." Ignorant of Section's plans for Chandler, she nonetheless exacts her own form of justice. Still, by

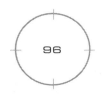

the end of the hour it's clear this episode has been less an opportunity for titillation than it has been a cold lesson for Nikita in Section's trademark cruelty and manipulation of its operatives' weaknesses.

Music

"Watch Me Fall" by **SIANspheric** on *Somnium* (Sonic Unyon) — opening scene with balloons

"In Your Life" by **Clove** on *Rollercoaster* (Nebula Records) — Nikita walking with Chandler

"All Dressed Up in San Francisco" by **Philosopher Kings** on *Philosopher Kings* (Sony Music Canada) — Nikita in the mall

"Jersey Girl" by **Holly Cole Trio** on *Temptation* (Alert Music/Metro Blue) — Nikita dancing with Chandler

"Secret" by **Tristan Psionic** on *TPA Flight 028* (Sonic Unyon) — confrontation between Michael and Chandler

Guest Cast

Simon MacCorkindale (Alec Chandler), Michael Filipowich (Kosten)

103 LOVE

Written by Michael Loceff
Directed by Jon Cassar

Nikita and Michael pose as a husband-and-wife mercenary team to get close to an arms dealer who has stolen a deadly nerve gas on behalf of terrorist group Red Cell.

This fan favorite was the first episode of the series to be filmed. According to producer Joel Surnow, the first three episodes were filmed in reverse order to shake up the cast and crew and to work out any bugs before the pilot was shot. What he got was strong

L — Inside Union Station, Front Street
S — Sage and Peter arrive

L — Union Station, Front Street
S — Peter and Sage are picked up
   in the limo

Bottom right:
L — Rear of 11 King Street West at
   Melinda Street
S — The "DeAnza Building"

Below:
L — Melinda Street, near King and Yonge
S — Bauer and his crew arrive

performances all round. Wilson and Dupuis's chemistry was imme-diate and palpable.

With a great script from Michael Loceff, peppered with "Section-speak" and gadgets that would make James Bond's Q jealous, many of the supporting players get juicy scenes. Alberta Watson nails her character, Madeline, from the get go. There is no question that Madeline is a ruthless yet insightful judge of human behavior, and Watson's quick circle of the interrogation room is almost humorous in its efficiency. Don Francks imbues Walter with humanity and warmth as he and Wilson connect in the ongoing flirt-a-thon. Guest actor Tobin Bell, well known for his portrayal of villains in both film and television, proves Bauer to be a worthy adversary for Section and gives the audience one of the series' most memorable villains.

Among the many standout scenes, director Jon Cassar gives us two particularly memorable ones. Cassar and director of photography Danny Nowak create a powerful tag scene in which a disgusted Nikita aims her gun at Section's shocking new bedfellow, the loathsome Bauer. Nikita's schoolgirl outfit belies her feral impulse to exact

L — Union Station, stairs to the train platforms
S — Nikita and Michael try to locate the chemical weapon

revenge. But the real gem is a still moment for Peta Wilson, as Nikita waits among the trees outside Bauer's compound. She visibly relaxes and steals a moment to feed her soul as she closes her eyes and turns her face sunward. The series is punctuated by moments like these where Wilson offers us a glimpse inside Nikita's reality and the price she pays for her life inside Section.

Peta Wilson is great in this episode and rises to the challenge of exposing many facets of her onscreen alter ago. Whether it's playing the gum-cracking brat of act one, the capable operative with feline moves taking on Bauer, or a woman conflicted, she proves herself to be astute, versatile, and vulnerable.

Music

"Night of the King Snake" by **Big Rude Jake** on *Blue Pariah* (independent) — Peter and Sage arrive

"Expression of Loneliness" by **Moonsocket** on *The Best Thing* (Sappy Records) — Nikita at Bauer's gate and end song

"Hey Man Nice Shot" by **Filter** on *Short Bus* (Warner Bros) — bomb sequence

"News" by **Clove** on *Rollercoaster* (Nebula Records) — searching the train station

"Still Waitin'" by **Big Sugar** on *Five Hundred Pounds* (Silvertone) — Michael and Nikita dancing

"Standing Around Crying" by **Big Sugar** on *Five Hundred Pounds* (Silvertone) — Nikita's striptease

Guest Cast

Tobin Bell (Bauer), Valerie Boyce (Stephanie), James Gallanders (Ornett), Blaine Joseph Bray (Andy)

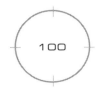
104 SIMONE

Written by Michael Loceff
Directed by Jerry Ciccoritti

Nikita poses as a recruit for the eccentric, high-tech terrorist group Glass Curtain, which has been cultivating new members over the Internet. Once inside, however, Nikita discovers a captive Section One operative: Michael's wife, Simone, who was thought to have been dead for more than three years.

Michael Loceff gives us another strong story line, this time filling in back story on Michael and offering one of the more eccentric villains of the series, Errol Sparks, (Julian Richings revels in his over-the-top character.) Director Jerry Ciccoritti and director of photography Danny Nowak experiment effectively with several new looks. The four-square split-screen effect works nicely to convey the noise and chaos of the video games room. The stretchy-cam technique used in the episode's climax communicates both the urgency of the operatives' race against the clock as they evacuate the bunker and the surreal horror of Michael's second loss of Simone.

Unfortunately there is no depth given to Simone or the effect of her loss and no time spent establishing why she'd choose suicide over freedom, so it is left to Dupuis to do all the work. The episode gives him the opportunity to flex his dramatic muscles as we watch Michael's control begin to unravel. His best moments are with Wilson as Nikita plays friend and therapist. The actors take the spaces between the words and make a dance out of the silence. Dupuis has a remarkable capacity to communicate volumes with just his eyes, and his stillness is frequently the perfect foil for Wilson's activity. Early in the series, the producers and Dupuis disagreed on just how much emotion Michael would convey, but by the third and fourth episodes, feedback indicated that the audience got it, and the actor was vindicated.

Although it's not explicitly stated, one is left with the impression

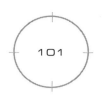

that not only does Operations know Simone is being held captive by Glass Curtain but has known all along. It's a notion that, for the audience, serves to expand the scope of Section's machinations. Michael may be the golden boy, but Operations will not flinch at using his loyalty to serve his own ends.

The episode is framed by scenes with Nikita and her neighbor Carla, a relationship that provides a healthy contrast to Nikita's other dysfunctional female-female relationship, with Madeline — and with her own mother, as we will learn. This girl-pal friendship does much to normalize Nikita's life and to round out her frames of reference. Although there are surprises in store for the audience, the relationship gives Wilson and the writers room to humanize Nikita.

Music

"Chorus" and "Recitative" by **Christoph William Gluck** — classical pieces used throughout the episode

"Red Zone" by **Mark Stewart** on *Control Data* (Mute/Warner Special Products) — in the arcade

"Slacker Boy Blue" by **Katrocket** on *The Town Disguised as a City* (Hoodwink Records) — Nikita and Carla talking

Guest Cast

Mung-Ling Tsui (Simone), Julian Richings (Sparks), Ingrid Veninger (Siobhan)

105 FRIEND

Written by Naomi Janzen
Directed by Guy Magar

Nikita attempts to protect a childhood friend, Julie, from Section while preventing the assassination of a visiting politician involved in peace talks.

L — The Hangar,
Downsview
airport
(Sheppard Avenue
and Allen Road)
S — Nikita spots
"Julie"

This memorable episode from Naomi Janzen (who will give us another strong female-centered story with "Mother") is important as the first story told completely within the dramatic logic of La Femme Nikita. Producer Joel Surnow singles out "Friend" because it does not draw from the series' big-screen origins, nor does it act as another straight-ahead action and spy piece. "Friend" is also the first of many episodes in which Nikita risks her life by breaking Section protocols to protect an innocent.

Wilson does a fine job here, entering the drama pissed off and uncharacteristically short-tempered with Walter. She imparts a real sense that the character's life goes on before and after the cameras roll. The story also offers her and guest actor Marnie McPhail (Julie) the welcome opportunity to display the closeness shared between two women friends and the ferocity of two trained killers facing off. The showdown confirms an essential difference between Nikita and her targets: Nikita fights because she has no choice, whereas Julie fights for a cause in which she believes. Yet self-definition is problematic as Julie defines herself by her job while Nikita fights to maintain her identity in spite of it. McPhail does a wonderful job as Julie, taking her from the afraid-of-her-own-shadow mouse to the woman slowly realizing the real implications of having to leave everything and everyone in her life to the soulless killing machine of the finale.

There are also some clever spy and action elements to the episode. In the torture scene, straight out of *Lethal Weapon* 2, Peta Wilson is like a drowning cat that refuses to give up one of her nine lives. Nikita proves herself a worthy adversary to her torturers — not only in body but in spirit — with her retort to her interrogator's "praise" that she has the courage of a man: "How would you know?" Director Guy Magar gives us a couple of exciting and compact action sequences as Nikita slides backward on her back across the floor (Hong Kong action-film style), shooting at an assassin in an overhead air vent, while Michael breaks through a second-story window, shooting and killing Nikita's torturer while making his descent. Whew!

In this episode, Nikita spends a lot of time hiding: hiding behind glasses, behind her bangs, behind an all-too-transparent noncha-lance, hiding evidence of the assassins trailing Mijovich, and hiding her friend Julie. Michael's behavior extends this voyeuristic theme of watching and being watched. He lifts her sunglasses to read the truth in Nikita's eyes but fails to find Julie in Nikita's apartment. Michael also creates a cover story to hide Nikita's failure to discover the truth about Julie's identity. As a Section One operative, though, Nikita is still very green; as clever as she is to forestall Julie's execution by Section One, she misses the collision of coincidences that leads to her own capture and torture by the Legion. Julie confirms what we already know about Section's visibility.

Music

"Night of the Iguana" by **Huevos Rancheros** on *Get Outta Dodge* (Mint) — Julie and Nikita at the bar
"Last Playboy Interview" by **Merlin's** on *Merlin Arcade* (Channel 3 Records) — Nikita and Julie play dress-up

Guest Cast

Marnie McPhail (Julie), David Calderisi (Jovan Mijovich), Billy Otis (Harry), Joseph Scoren (Tiko)

106 TREASON

Written by Robert Cochran
Directed by Jerry Ciccoritti

Nikita is again protector of the innocent as she seeks to rescue a fellow operative's son who has been kidnapped. The kidnapper, Suba, is a traitorous CIA contact who has begun smuggling waste uranium out of the United States.

In "Treason" we get a good Section One story in which the Section's political goals interlace with Nikita's personal goals. The hour show-cases Nikita's growing confidence, particularly in the scene where, dismissed by Michael, she tells Operations she can deliver Suba. And it is Nikita, not Michael, who determines that Roger has betrayed the team when the first mission fails.

Visually, the episode has some interesting moments. Ciccoritti's stretchy cam is employed to no significant end. But, along with

L — The Guvernment Night Club (132 Queens Quay East)
S — Michael rescues Nikita from Suba
(the club's interior, including the dramatic red entranceway, has been used in several episodes)

director of photography Michael Storey, the director does create a particularly effective and memorable scene at the farmhouse during the first raid. Imaginative lighting and a stylish mix of video, film, and hand-held camera work convey the stress, chaos, and claustrophobia of the raid and ambush.

There is some nice scripting from Robert Cochran, who uses humor to deflate a couple of trite television conventions: Nikita, a vision in lavender Lycra, infiltrates Suba's club as a call girl delayed by a philosophy exam, and Michael, in a delightful comic turn by Dupuis, extricates Nikita as damsel in distress by posing as her jealous, irate husband.

Peter Outerbridge gives a solid performance as Roger, the first in a long line of "red shirt" types (as with *Star Trek* episodes when the new guy in the red jersey is killed off before the show's end). And although we really don't end up caring about the plight of little kidnapped Kyle, Roger's "cancellation" is shocking. That he not only retained his humanity but hid the existence of a son from Section speaks to the organization's fallibility.

This episode is framed by strong Nikita–Madeline scenes. It begins with a humorous thrust-and-parry between the two women, undercut by a chilling reminder from Madeline that Section will require an even greater standard of performance from Nikita. It ends with a tearful Nikita, having forgotten her earlier resolve to remain inscrutable, vainly seeking answers and even comfort from her ruthless overseer.

Music

"La Cumbia, La Cumbia" by **Diego Marujanda** (HMV/Festival Records) — dancing in the bar

"La Noche" by **Diego Marujanda** (HMV/Festival Records) — Nikita in Suba's back room

"Red" by **Sister Machine Gun** on Burn (TVT Records) — Nikita tries to rescue Kyle

Guest Cast

Peter Outerbridge (Roger), Von Flores (Suba), Noah Reid (Kyle)

107 MOTHER

Written by Naomi Janzen
Directed by Guy Magar

Nikita goes undercover again, this time as the long-lost daughter of a ruthless arms dealer, Helen Wicke, who, along with her equally cold-blooded husband, John, is preparing to sell a nuclear trigger.

Director Guy Magar and writer Naomi Janzen team up again to give us a story that examines the most fundamental of female-female relationships, that of mother and daughter. The narrative relies on the suspension of disbelief by both characters. Helen wants to believe she has found her daughter and "plays" at dressing her up, attempting to compress all the lost years into a short few days. In a wonderful piece of casting, the elegant Sherry Miller conveys with perfection the fragility of Helen's newfound conviction. Nikita needs Helen to believe, but she, too, is yearning for a relationship she never had. By the final act we learn the depth of abandonment she feels. Wilson and Miller hold the tension of their characters' desires beautifully.

"Mother" is an important episode because it establishes Nikita as a true Section operative. She executes John to avenge another agent's death and is somehow resigned to her fate as a pawn in Section mind games. There is a rather horrifying pattern emerging in her relationship with Michael, as well. When she is beaten she is "doing her job" and is rewarded with approval (even Madeline is waiting by her hospital bedside). Further, although these incidents may be orchestrated by Operations, they are carried out by Michael and are the only occasions that evoke any overt tenderness from him. There seems to be no limit to the kind of hell the writers can put Nikita through without losing the audience. This is dark stuff, but it will get even darker before season's end.

Music

Original music by Sean Callery

Guest Cast

Sherry Miller (Helen Wicke), Wayne Best (John Wicke)

108 ESCAPE

Written by Andrew Deltman & Daniel Truly
Directed by George Bloomfield

Nikita is approached by another Section One operative who offers her the hope of escape. Her suspicions that her loyalty is being tested are compounded when Michael begins to seduce her.

This hour is built on a terrific idea: what if Nikita is forced to choose between her freedom and a relationship with Michael? Strong direction from George Bloomfield and superb cast performances rescue a plot so full of holes one could drive a mobile-com van through it!

Nikita doesn't know that Eric (whose name we don't learn until the end of the third act) works in Section. As soon as they've met, however, he shows up in the command center and on Nikita's next two missions. If her suspicions were not aroused, *his* should have been.

The presence of surveillance equipment in Nikita's apartment is not surprising, but it does raise questions about the logic of previous story lines (especially "Friend"), and it makes the apartment a

Above left:
L — Berkeley Castle courtyard
S — Eric approaches Nikita

Above right:
L — Berkeley Castle, The Esplanade
    and Hahn Place
S — Nikita's apartment

Left:
L — Varsity Stadium, Bloor Street
    and Bedford Road
S — mission to rescue prisoners

Above:
L — Fire escape inside courtyard of
   Berkeley Castle
S — Staircase from which Eric observes Nikita

Above right:
L — Varsity Stadium, exterior

Right:
L — Varsity Stadium, under the bleachers
S — Nikita hears an enemy agent

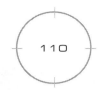

questionable setting for Michael's seduction of Nikita. In fact, the whole episode is so riddled with red flags one wonders how she ever believed his advances. Dupuis has an extraordinary ability to convey, just with his eyes, regret, pain, and heartbreak, even as Michael is delivering the crushing emotional blow to Nikita in the final act. Peta Wilson is equally heartbreaking as she allows waves of vulnerability, realization, and devastation to wash across her face.

The seduction scenes have made this episode another fan favorite in spite of its flaws, and the now famous "hand dance" is even more sexually charged than the pair's lovemaking in "Hard Landing." The onscreen chemistry between the two leads is undeniable. Another powerful visual is the meeting of light and dark in the staged exchange between Madeline and Nikita as the topic of Michael's emotional life is discussed. Alberta Watson's performance as the beguiling Madeline is fascinating. Even as she steers Nikita along pre-determined paths she exudes warmth and concern through eyes that can go dead in an instant. And then there is the unforgettable coming-of-age moment for Nikita, easily one of the best scenes of the series, as she storms into Section, hair wild like a lion's mane, and delivers the surveillance equipment ripped out of the apartment, drywall still attached. She calls Operations' bluff and leaves the trio behind: Operations amused, Madeline approving, and Michael unreadable.

Music

"Evidence" by **Tara MacLean** on *Silence* (Nettwerk /Sony Music Canada) — Nikita working out

"Torn" by **Rose Chronicles** on *Happily Ever After* (Nettwerk) — Nikita thinking about Michael

"Temple" by **Beverly Klass** on *III* (Boxx Entertainment) — Michael seducing Nikita

"Cun Lacoudhir" by **Rhea Obsession** on *Initiation* (Spider Records) — Michael and Nikita dancing

Guest Cast

Jaimz Woolvett (Eric), Anais Granofsky (Carla), Domenic Cuzzocrea (Cassian), Philip Williams (Jerico Perez)

109 GRAY

Written by Robert Cochran
Directed by Ken Girotti

Michael travels to Prague to bid for the return of the Section's stolen directory, but when the thief is killed by another buyer, Benko, the file is nowhere to be found. Section focuses their interest on Gray Wellman, a bus passenger on whom the thief may have planted the file.

"Gray" is a good, straight-ahead spy story that prepares the way for the more relationship-oriented follow-up episode, "Choice." Nikita's booby-trapped necklace, fully equipped with microphone and explosives, is a great *Mission Impossible* James Bond gadget that effectively reminds us of the spy element of the series. The imaginative resolution, whereby Section simulates Gray and Nikita's conversation and stages a phony explosion of the necklace, is given a nice *Nikita* twist. Nikita grabs Benko when he realizes he's been deceived, tying his fate to hers if he presses the detonator. It's a daring move — even Michael is concerned — but in the end Nikita's bluff works; she recovers the detonator, and *almost* hands it over to Michael. That she changes her mind and keeps the device is a loaded gesture and a memorable moment: she is intent on retaining control over her death, her life, her destiny, her identity, and her soul.

Other characters in the series are emerging, as well. Michael's skills as a strategist come to the fore: he suggests using Gray, an innocent, to lure Benko into the open. Section may not get the directory, but they can get the other buyer (removing that potential threat) and

L — Osgoode Hall
(Queen Street and University Avenue)
S — Michael arrives in Prague

Inset:
L — Doorway to Osgoode Hall
S — Michael meets with Harding and Benko

capture an enemy at the same time. As in "Charity," Madeline coun-sels Michael on his relationship with Nikita. In light of later story developments, it is difficult to discern if this is observation or manip-ulation on Madeline's part, but Michael's appearance in the shadows across from Gray's house feeds the jealousy theory that Nikita will espouse at the conclusion of "Choice." Madeline's foray into the field is a rarity, as she poses as a cop (M. Frayn) and questions Gray at the local police station. Equally rare is the suggestion that Section works in cooperation with local authorities (a theme that will be developed further in "Voices"). In a lighter moment, Alberta Watson and Peta Wilson have some fun playing up the sexual innuendo of their discussion of Gray's cooking skills, emphasizing Nikita's increasing comfort around Madeline as she becomes more settled into Section.

Music

"Tsunami" by **Guru Stefan** on MOYOM — *Beyond* (Hybrid Structure) — Michael arrives in Prague

"Howling" by **Morcheeba** on *Who Can You Trust?* (Warner Music) — Nikita is wired

Guest Cast

Callum Keith Rennie (Gray), James Kidnie (Benko), David Jansen (Harding), Carlo Rota (Mick Schtoppel)

Clockwise from top left:
L — Reverse angle of doorway to Osgoode Hall
      (looking down York Street)
S — view behind Michael as he meets with Harding and Benko

L — Liberty Street and Fraser Avenue
S — Michael arrives to meet Harding

L — Pardee and Liberty Streets
S — Michael searches Harding's body for the disk

L — Lamport Stadium, south side of Liberty Street and
      Hardee Avenue
S — Harding gets off the bus to meet Michael

L — Holy Trinity Church
      (Trinity Square on West side of the Eaton's Centre)
S — Nikita and Gray go for a walk

Top three photos:
L — Nathan Phillips Square
    (Queen Street East)
S — Gray and Nikita walk through
    the square

Bottom:
L — Nathan Phillips Square
S — "Nikita's" collar explodes

110 CHOICE

Written by Michael Loceff
Directed by George Bloomfield

The relationship between Nikita and Gray continues to develop but Nikita soon finds it impossible to balance a private life filled with lies and Section's demands.

"Choice" plays out the question (and answer) of why Nikita cannot have a meaningful outside relationship. It also suggests the reason ruthless killers are recruited or created by Section. The job of an operative is to kill or be killed. Relationships inside Section seem to end in death, and relationships with outsiders don't work because of all the deception required. The assassination from the hotel suite marks the turning point for Nikita and Gray in this respect, and it is the last action sequence from the original Luc Besson film to make its way into the series. Loceff also creates the wonderful scene in the mall to emphasize Nikita's lesson. While minding Casey, Gray's young daughter, Nikita is called in for a mission. Distracted for a few seconds, she loses the child and experiences every mother's nightmare. The added twist for Nikita is that her absence from the mission queers the deal, shooting begins, and lives are lost.

Madeline's description of the outside world as an illusion is apt, and her statement that the people in Section are "ghosts" could be straight out of a good spy novel. In contrast to this very practical but cynical advice is the voice of the humanist, Walter, who tells Nikita not to mourn what she cannot have but to sing the tune she can. She can live with Section rules or she can live in spite of them. It's a lovely moment that underlines the real choice of the story.

Music

"Death by Moonlight" by **Rhea Obsession** on Initiation (Spider Records) — opening scene

Above:
L — Sunnyside Pavilion
  (Lakeshore Boulevard West)
S — opening ripoff takes place inside
  the courtyard (this location was
  also used in "Old Habits")

Top right:
L — Queen's Quay subway terminal,
  Harbourfront
S — Nikita loses Casey

Middle:
L — Spinnaker's Restaurant at Harbourfront
(207 Queen's Quay West)
S — Nikita, Gray, and Casey have lunch

Bottom:
L — East Liberty Street
S — Michael takes down Price

"Drown" by **Vibrolux** on *Vibrolux* (independent) — Nikita descends into computer room

Guest Cast

Callum Keith Rennie (Gray), Robert Bockstael (Price), Joseph Griffin (Valery)

111 RESCUE

Written by Peter Bellwood
Directed by Ken Girotti

The team is sent to Russia to blow up a chemical weapons plant, but Michael is wounded and left behind during the escape. He finds shelter with a nurse from a local hospital, while Madeline and Nikita seek to effect a rescue before he is discovered by the secret police.

"Rescue" opens with one of the most beautifully constructed and most memorable sequences in the series. David Thompson's inspired editing demonstrates the power of one piece of music, perfectly employed. The show has hit its stride after some experimentation with style; the overuse of nonoriginal music in the first few episodes is now balanced by a focused use of band music to supplement Sean Callery's moody original scores.

An all-too-common flaw in North American television can be the characterization of non-Westerners. In this episode we get cartoon Russians invoking the memory of Rambo to understand their political enemy and decrying "Western decadence." As adept as Nigel Bennett (Petrosian) is at playing charming villains (his Lacroix of *Forever Knight* was delicious), he cannot redeem the portrayal of the Russians as one-dimensional buffoons running about in circles. (To add insult to injury, the most clever of them turns out to be a Section One deep cover agent in the end.) A more worthy and legitimate opponent most certainly

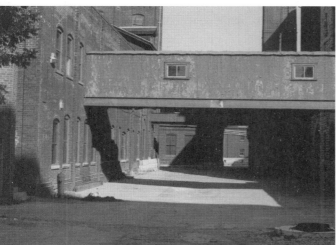

Left from top:

L — Richard Hearn Thermal
    Generating Station
    (440 Unwin Avenue)
S — the hospital where Angie
    works

L — Gooderham and Worts
    Distillery
S — Madeline hotwires a car

L — Gooderham and Worts
    Distillery
S — the street outside Angie's
    apartment (reverse angle)

Below:
L — Richard Hearn Thermal
    Generating Station
    (440 Unwin Avenue)
S — The chemical plant is
    destroyed by Michael's team

Nancy Beatty holds up the Gemini she won for her performance in "Rescue."

would have upped the stakes and increased the dramatic tension.

Fortunately, there are real gems to be found in the scenes between Michael and the nurse, Angie. Dupuis and Nancy Beatty, who won a Gemini Award for her role, deliver performances that are relaxed, real, and subtle. Dupuis's minimalist approach for Michael is a perfect fit with Beatty's naturalism. A little dialogue goes a long way in the skillful hands of these performers, satisfying the maxim "show it, don't tell it." Angie's homespun philosophy speaks directly to Nikita's situation: the nail that stands up gets hammered. One lovely moment occurs when Madeline catches Angie looking at Michael with Nikita, but the character ultimately receives short shrift when no one even checks to see if she is dead after she's been shot!

Writer Peter Bellwood does well exploiting the dramatic pairing of Nikita and Madeline. Watson and Bellwood keep Madeline unpredictable, giving her warm smiles when she tells Nikita the mission is on to rescue Michael, humor as she hot-wires a car, and a single-mindedness of purpose as she induces a heart attack to strengthen her cover. Madeline's ruthlessness is never in question, but her focus and self-control attain new levels in one (literally) heart-stopping moment. Her self-induced heart attack prefigures her eerie command of her autonomic functions in "Mandatory Refusal."

Music

"Beyond The Invisible" by **Enigma** on *Enigma 3: Le Roi est Mort, Vive le Roi* (EMD/Virgin) — opening sequence

Guest Cast

Nancy Beatty (Angie), Nigel Bennett (Petrosian), Diego Matamoros (Major Frankel), Waneta Storms (Nurse)

112 INNOCENT

Written by Michael Loceff
Directed by George Bloomfield

The innocent Nikita protects this time is a simpleminded pizza delivery man who stumbles into the middle of a terrorist plan to detonate a nuclear device in a highly populated city.

Loceff's script offers some interesting pairings: Nikita and Birkoff (giving us back story on Birkoff, exploiting the sibling-like relationship and developing their humorous banter), Rudy and Michael (the sharp contrast between Rudy's literalism and Michael's impenetrable seriousness is hilarious), and Rudy and Belinda (Bloomfield directs Traci Miller and Chaykin in a truly touching scene that is intimate, personal, and particular: a contrast to the series' signature high style).

"Innocent" succeeds largely because Maury Chaykin's performance as Rudy (for which he won a Gemini Award) is effortlessly funny and improvisational in style. Unfortunately the urgency of the political and nuclear threat is never really conveyed in a convincing

Maury Chaykin proudly displays the Gemini he won for the role of Rudy in "Innocent."

way. Conventional shots of the timer counting down are insufficient to compensate for a general lack of suspense. Proving the old adage that it is easier to care about the suffering of one person than a thousand, the truly tense moment presents itself when we believe, like Nikita, that Rudy is lost and the code needed to disarm the bomb has been lost along with him. That Operations would have the time (let alone that he would bother) to order Rudy's death during this "crisis" stretches believability to the limit.

L — corner of Yonge and Dundas streets
S — images shown while the clock chimes as the deadline is reached

Eugene Robert Glazer, however, does justice to a beautifully shot old-style spy meeting in the tradition of LeCarré or Deighton. An alley in the dead of night, the snow falling, green and purple lighting underscored by the band In The Nursery — all evoke the Cold War era. John Evans is completely credible as the slimy, weak traitor Guy Maygar, all spit and sobs as he spills the beans.

Music

"Precedent" by **In The Nursery** on *Deco* (ITN Corporation) — Operations and Guy meet

Guest Cast

Maury Chaykin (Rudy), John Evans (Maygar), Doru Bandol (Kassar), Traci Miller (Belinda)

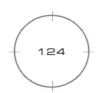

113 GAMBIT

Written by Michael Loceff
Directed by Jon Cassar

Section One must retrieve a stolen canister of Cobalt-60, but Madeline may have met her match when the thief she is interrogating has an uncanny insight into her past.

"Gambit" is a great cat-and-mouse episode that pits Madeline, a master profiler and ruthless interrogator, against Kessler, a master of disguise, a madman, and a terrorist who has eluded capture for 30 years. The show works well, balancing action and Section story lines with new character developments. Michael Loceff's clever script and Jon Cassar's imaginative directing (the episode was nominated for a Gemini Award) bring the wonderful Alberta Watson into the spotlight and illuminate Madeline's background.

The whole episode reads like a 101 course in master strategy. It begins with a visual sleight of hand in the teaser as we see Madeline doing what she does so well: conducting a ruthless interrogation. The twist, of course, is that all this is a VR simulation. Surprisingly, Madeline has to mentally prepare herself for the challenges of entering the mind set of her enemies, ferreting out their weaknesses and exploiting them. She appears to do all this at a cost.

In the mission brainstorming session we see the deductive processes that lead her to Kessler. Later, we watch Madeline dispassionately order and observe the death of an operative as Kessler makes his "escape," and we also see how Madeline uses Kessler's methods to bring him down. That Kessler knows Madeline, that he has either profiled her or gained access to her file again casts doubt upon the theory that Section One is "the most covert anti-terrorist group in the world."

David Thompson's editing again elevates the caliber of the storytelling as he lets the camera "discover" the death of the security man,

L — R. C. Harris Water Filtration Plant,
  2701 Queen Street East
S — University of Norway, Oslo, where Nikita picks up
  Annie

Hayes, and that of the abeyance operative in Kessler's interrogation room. With the stark lighting of Kessler's scenes in and out of Section, the video screen close-ups of his ransom message, the slow-motion camera work, and the reuse of the green and purple palette in lighting Kessler's lair, Director Jon Cassar and director of photography Michael McMurray expand and establish the visual repertoire and style of the series. At times the story and the visuals drift a little too close to *Silence of the Lambs*, but Harris Yulin's Kessler proves a worthy adversary, and the actor is delicious as he eyes the throat of his adversary from behind his Hannibal Lecter-style muzzle.

Nikita is in the background of this episode. But note the "bookend" scenes in which Madeline confesses her self-doubts to Nikita. As others have, Madeline feels secure exposing a vulnerability and confessing a weakness to Nikita. The final tag thus presents one of the more intriguing open endings of the season; we don't know if Nikita is being suggested as a younger Madeline, if the ice queen just feels the need to connect, or if this is all part of a larger plan to mold Nikita in her image.

Music

Original music by Sean Callery

Guest Cast

Harris Yulin (Kessler), Lindsey Connell (Annie), Todd William Schroeder (Shellen), Allan Murley (Hayes), John Ho (Janitor)

114 RECRUIT

Written by Larry Raskin
Directed by Reza Badiyi

No longer low man on the ladder, Nikita is assigned the final evaluation of a new recruit and must decide if the woman will live or die.

"Recruit" is a very strong Section story, full of psychological mine-fields, and it exposes more of the abuse and manipulation to which Nikita is subjected as she evolves as an operative. It is apparent early in the episode that the true subject of the evaluation is Nikita. Karyn's appeals to Nikita's sympathy are designed to remind us of Nikita's first day on the job. Michael's task is to cloud Nikita's judgment with feelings of jealousy. In true Michael style he takes it a step further: when Nikita asks him about the nature of his relationship with Karyn he asserts, "You should know me better than that by now." Why twist the truth once if you can twist it twice?

Karyn is played by Felicity Waterman, who coincidentally lost the lead in this series to Peta Wilson. However, her audition was so memorable that Joel Surnow promised her a guest spot and had her in mind when this script was written. Karyn's back story is that of the original big-screen Nikita, and this episode is the last direct tie to Luc Besson's film.

Nikita's development and maturity both as a member of Section One and as a human being are apparent here in her disinterest in being liked and playing idiotic games. But Nikita has built alliances within Section, which she manipulates to her advantage. The mood is lightened with a comic scene between Nikita and Birkoff, and their behavior is becoming more and more like that of a brother and sister. Nikita silently mouths Birkoff's "I don't do favors" line and employs her own brand of reverse psychology by suggesting the task she has in mind may be too difficult for him. Karyn and Nikita may be more alike than she would care to admit.

The episode offers a couple of surprises. Michael's shooting comes as a shock, especially at the hands of the cleverly cast middle-aged female bank teller. Just as shocking is Karyn's glee while she continues to shoot the already-dead enemy agents. Finally, that Nikita's big decision is not only moot but barely a blip in Operations' awareness makes her moral struggle insignificant.

Music

"Broken Man" by **SIANspheric** on *Somnium* (Sonic Unyon)
— Nikita thinking about Brian's death

Guest Cast

Felicity Waterman (Karyn), Markus Parilo (Brian), Jean Daigle (Kreizel), Denise Fergusson (Woman in Bank), Ted Whittall (Loan Officer), Greg Campbell (Drag Queen)

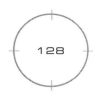

115 OBSESSED

Written by Robert Cochran
Directed by T.J. Scott

To secure a book containing a collection of damaging top-secret information, Nikita goes undercover as a trainer to the wife of Fanning, the brutal hit man who possesses it. Michael's mission is to seduce Lisa, the fragile and abused wife, thereby gaining access to Fanning's computer files.

T.J. Scott's sunny and light-filled episode is a real change of pace for *La Femme Nikita*. It gives Roy Dupuis the welcome opportunity to drop the stylized persona of Michael (not to mention his somber black clothing) and further establish his leading-man status and his considerable sexual appeal for the show's female audience. Michael's character is also given some room for growth. He is aware of the emotional paradox of exploiting Lisa's vulnerability in order to protect it. All too often he is Section's puppet, but here he makes a dangerous and private decision to balance the books by skimming some money from Fanning's accounts for Lisa. Not only does this act reveal a sense of justice previously unseen; it also reveals his professional acumen in embezzling the funds without leaving tracks for Section to follow.

Yvonne Scio fully captures the delicate nature of the abused and childlike Lisa. Low-angle camera shots of Fanning's heavy shoes reinforce the idea of a child's perspective, or at the very least that of a subservient. "#1 Crush," Garbage's song of obsessive love, sets the stage for Fanning's abusive, possessive relationship with his wife. Scott takes full advantage of Scio's beauty in the computer-theft scene, but it is a little overdone. She glides through the endless halls in flowing robes, every inch the romantic heroine in peril. We don't escape reality for long; Lisa's beating in the second act is brutal and all the more affecting because it is off-camera, allowing the viewer to imagine the worst. Lisa's pain is registered in the eyes of Matthew

WHAT'S IN A NAME?

One of the great challenges facing the *La Femme Nikita* writers can be that of naming all the new characters who pop up on each weekly episode. The writers often have to pick mundane or "common" names for characters to avoid potential legal hassles from individuals who might take exception at seeing a murderous sociopath on television with their name!

Often, inspiration comes from family, friends, or the *La Femme Nikita* crew itself. Several cases in point:

In "Not Was," Michael's cover name is Mr. Bonnière, the name of one of *La Femme Nikita*'s frequent guest directors. And Karen Perez, a location manager, won the dubious distinction of lending her name to Michael's torturer in the same episode.

In "Innocent," a terrorist named Kassar threatens to blow up a city with a nuclear device. Jon Cassar is one of the series regular guest directors.

In "I Remember Paris," the gallery owner is named Matteo after Rocco Matteo, the production designer.

Ackerman from "Hard Landing" is named after Dave Ackerman, the series' dolly grip, while Wallace from "All Good Things" is named after Mark Wallace, the 1st assistant director.

In some cases the actors themselves provide their own names, as was the case with Natalie (Persad) and Frank (Bishun) in "Not Was."

Finally, lists of crew names often cycle through Birkoff's computer screens.

So next time you're watching, take a few minutes, hit the pause button on the vcr or read the series' credits. You just might see the name of tonight's villain or new operative!

Ferguson and Roy Dupuis as they listen from Section's command center. Her suicide attempt is entirely consistent, as Scio makes it wholly believable that Lisa thinks she somehow deserves the abuse she is suffering at the hands of Nikita and Michael.

Nikita takes a back seat for most of the episode, but even she is not immune to Section manipulation. The mission also seems designed to provoke a jealous response from Nikita, doubtless a handy secondary benefit for Section management. But what fan doesn't get a huge kick out of Nikita beating the snot out of Fanning? One of *La Femme Nikita*'s great attractions: wish fulfillment by proxy.

Music

"#1 Crush" by **Garbage** from *Romeo and Juliet Soundtrack* (Capitol Records/Alamo) — wedding scene

"Woman" by **In The Nursery** on *Deco* (ITN Corporation) — love scene

Guest Cast

Yvonne Scio (Lisa Fanning), Douglas O'Keeffe (David Fanning)

116 MISSING

Written by Naomi Janzen
Directed by Reza Badiyi

Secrets within secrets as Operations plays Nikita and Michael against each other. Nikita is told that one of their targets in an upcoming mission is actually Operations' son and her mission is to keep him alive at all costs without Michael's knowledge. Meanwhile, Michael acts on Operations' behalf to protect him from Nikita's blackmail bid for freedom.

Scriptwriter Naomi Janzen returns to examine the theme of parent and child. This time it is Operations who seeks to protect a son he cannot acknowledge. The son, Steven, has ironically become a target for Section because he is funding his lifelong search for his MIA father by selling classified information and goods to terrorists. As Roger's plight in "Treason" has already established how Section handles the security risks posed by the existence of family members, Operations' fear for his son's safety is legitimate, and his choice to remain unknown to Steven is wise.

Operations' relationship with Nikita is a complicated one. In seeking out her help he unconsciously acknowledges the value of her eccentricities (read compassion) within the organization. Nikita is learning to take advantage of an opportunity, but she hasn't yet acquired the poker face she'll need. In a bid for freedom she takes control of the use of surveillance to gain the upper hand, but the freedom she longs for won't be handed over — she will have to take it — and she stands up to Operations fiercely and fearlessly. There is

L — College Street and Euclid Avenue
S — Nikita contacts Steven Wolfe and the team

something of a Pygmalion moment in Nikita's assertion, "I've paid for your bloody deportment classes a hundred times over." One wonders just how many Professor Higginses she has had to endure.

Although Nikita is able to protect Michael while faking Steven's death, she is unable to have her cake and eat it, too, when it comes to her bargain with the devil. Operations, aware of Nikita's plan to protect herself, sends Michael to spy on her. Michael is cast once again in the role of errand boy and, as in "Recruit," he again makes careless mistakes: Steven catches him reloading during the shoot-out.

Not only do we get Operations' back story, but we get a story very close to Eugene Robert Glazer's heart. He has long been interested in the plight of American soldiers missing in action since the Vietnam War. His research on the subject informed the character "bible" he developed for the Operations character, and he is writing a screenplay on the subject. Throughout the series, Glazer can be spotted wearing a POW MIA pin.

Glazer is heartbreaking as Operations listens with a mixture of pride and pain to his son's story of loss. It goes a long way to humanizing a character so mysterious that he has no name until the end of Season Two. Peta Wilson offers some neat physical bits as she hops across the cold floor when awoken by Operations in the middle of the night. Her double-take at the peephole is priceless.

Music

"Hanging On A Curtain" by **Morphine** on *Like Swimming* (Rykodisc) — Nikita hides the video of Operations

Guest Cast

Christopher Kennedy (Steven), Dan Pawlick (Shirov), Tony Nappo (Dean), Pedro Salvin (Bagot), Harper Quantrill (Borsos)

117 NOISE

Written by Michael Loceff
Directed by T. J. Scott

Birkoff comes under fire from all sides when a mission is breached and he is forced to kill his attacker. The trauma of this first kill paralyses Birkoff with fear, and he is placed in abeyance, but Nikita steps in to help him face his fears and avoid cancellation.

This is the fifth episode that focuses on Wilson's fellow cast members. Matthew Ferguson shines as agoraphobic cyber-geek and mission analyst Seymour Birkoff. He hides behind his monitor and digital readouts, and it has never occurred to him that the violence of the real world could reach him. His first mobile assignment becomes a trial by fire when an enemy agent shoots up the van from which he is direct-ing a mission. Birkoff, we learn, has lied about killing his sister (both to Nikita and Section) — but why? One has to wonder if *any* of the main characters fit the usual profile required for entry into Section: that of a cold-blooded murderer. If he didn't kill anyone, just how did Birkoff end up in Section?

L — Looking north on Cherry Street, near Commissioners Street
S — Mission van en route to rescue Michael's team

In addition to building the brother-sister relationship between Nikita and Birkoff, this episode reinforces the value of Birkoff's unique gifts by introducing Simon, a less-than-effective Birkoff

L — Unwin Avenue, Toronto Dock Area
S — Nikita and Birkoff rescue Michael's team

wannabe. Tara Slone also joins the cast as Gail, a fellow computer geek
and love interest for Seymour. Typically, Birkoff and Operations have
the thankless task of delivering most of the exposition for the show.
"Missing" and "Noise" (and "Gambit," in the case of Madeline) represent the first important steps in exploiting the complexities of these
underused characters.

Costume Designer Laurie Drew outdoes herself with a funky pink
outfit for Nikita in the opening sequence, an impossibly small red
dress (made from one piece of material cut on the bias), a regal shirt
coat, and the long lines of a pinstripe pantsuit. Set Designer Rocco
Matteo's club sets have always been wonderful eye candy, and the art
gallery with its body-art dancers is unforgettable. Birkoff's apartment
deep in the heart of Section is a visual essay on pop culture, with its
blow-up plastic furniture, Japanese animé artwork, proliferation of
computer and television monitors, and the "tulip chair," which will
migrate from here to the observation room and later to Nikita's apartment. "Noise" garnered *La Femme Nikita* three nominations for
Canadian Gemini Awards: Laurie Drew for costume design, Rocco
Matteo for production design, and Matthew Ferguson for acting.

The mission van, which the author found parked behind the LFN studios in Mississauga.

Music

"Tape Loop" by **Morcheeba** on *Who Can You Trust?* (Warner Music/ China Records) — Nikita in the nightclub

"Inion/Daughter" by **Afro-Celt Sound System** on *Afro-Celt Sound System: Vol. 1 – Sound Magic* (Real World) — Michael planting tracking devices on weapons

Guest Cast

Richard Waugh (Simon), Vieslav Krystyan (Golden), Jon Wildman (Lonnie), Angela Vint (Ginger), Tara Slone (Gail)

118 VOICES

Written by Maurice Hurley
Directed by David Warry-Smith

Real life and Section life intersect when Nikita fends off an attack by Crane, a serial rapist-murderer. Led by a witness's description, a police detective cracks Nikita's cover, exposing himself and Nikita to cancellation.

In a story that springs from the dramatic conceit of Luc Besson's *La*

Above:
L — Victoria College, 91 Charles Street West
S — The Embassy

Top:
L — Pratt Library, 71 Queens Park Crescent East
S — Nikita and Michael stake out the Embassy

Below:
L — Queens Park, north side
S — Nikita and Michael stake out the Embassy

L — Reverse angle of the parking lot behind
     Kelly Library, University of Toronto
S — Nikita is observed beating up Crane

L — Behind the Kelly Library
     (University of Toronto),
     113 Joseph Street
S — Crane attacks Nikita

L — Canary Restaurant on Cherry Street
S — Crane exits the diner and enters the building next door

Femme Nikita we witness another difficult stage in Nikita's growth as an agent. In attempting to handle her exposure to the police without help from Section, she endangers the life of a police detective, sympathetically played by the scruffy, handsome Stephen Shellen (*A River Runs Through It, Rude*). But it's an awkward lesson. How can she trust Section not to cancel him? The idea that they might have given the cop what he wanted never occurs to her, but why should it? Accommodation has never been Section's strong suit.

Nikita is learning about another aspect of life inside Section, and also about what happens when reality and life within Section cross paths. It is an effectively jarring moment when O'Brian walks into the middle of a mission in progress. (The moment in the gallery also affords the director an irresistible visual pun as Nikita, pretty as a picture, is shot through an oversized frame in the gallery. Too bad the detective has no idea she will be framing him for the rapist's murder by the hour's end!)

As in "Obsessed," Nikita gets to beat the crap out of the villain (her would-be rapist), vicariously affording the female audience another shot at wish fulfillment. And in a parallel men-are-shits story line, Carla's new boyfriend puts the moves on Nikita. A little obvious, but it brings the welcome return of Anais Gronofsky and of real life for Nikita.

Unfortunately, in the end we don't know enough about the detective to really care about his fate. The fact that she's put a cop's life in danger provokes the cold shoulder from Nikita's work colleagues, but it is not enough to create a connection with the audience. It is an interesting departure that Operations pushes Nikita to fix the mess she's made. Her solution (framing the detective and offering him prison or a new job with Section) is classic Section S.O.P., and Madeline's chilling observation hits the mark as she declares that Nikita has finally become "one of us."

Music

"Mandra" by **In The Nursery** on *Deco* (ITN Corporation) — Tossi under surveillance

"Ground" by **Vibrolux** on *Vibrolux* (independent) — Nikita, Carla, and boyfriend at dinner

"The Stars Above" by **SIANspheric** on *Somnium* (Sonic Unyon) — Nikita comforts Carla/Madeline talks to Nikita

Guest Cast

Stephen Shellen (O'Brian), Anais Granofsky (Carla), Oliver Becker (Jack Crane)

119 WAR

Written by Maurice Hurley
Directed by René Bonnière

Section One's directory has been cracked, operatives are being executed worldwide, and Section is at war with Red Cell, who have captured and tortured Nikita and Michael. When Michael declares his love to Nikita and she gives up information to save his life, she becomes the unwitting victim of a cruel manipulation designed to lead Red Cell into a trap.

The other shoe has finally dropped. The directory that disappeared in "Gray" has been recovered by Red Cell. And what a formidable enemy they will prove themselves to be over the course of the series. The wonderful James Faulkner (*I Claudius*, Joel Surnow's *Covington Cross*) proves a most worthy adversary in the person of the Inquisitor as he gleefully plays with his victims' darkest fears. A Gothic counterpart to Section's Madeline, he fails to break Nikita's spirit initially, despite his horrific torture technique.

The episode is an exploration of the ruthless politics of survival,

Section-style. If the trap for Red Cell fails, any and all Section survivors will be exterminated by the agency. This glimpse of the larger organizational philosophy that has informed Operations' and Madeline's management style puts the maladjusted, warped reality of Section into a new perspective. It speaks to Nikita's strength that Operations, Madeline, and Michael invent such cruel lies to get her to crack. The story is not just about personal survival, but corporate survival.

Nikos Evdemon begins a lengthy stay with the show as director of photography, and with director René Bonnière creates a dark and disturbing episode with visual references straight out of Orwell's 1984. Once again the sadomasochistic note sounds as Maurice Hurley's script juxtaposes violence and torture with love and compassion. Bonnière has been singled out by Wilson as a favorite guest director; their work on scenes requiring intense or complex emotions are some of the series' best.

Michael's fear that he will dishonor himself fuels the image of Michael as a knight. Dupuis is marvelous in the tender exchanges with Peta Wilson and even more so in the final scene as he stands in the white hospital room, shamed and devastated by his manipulations and the real cost of his betrayal. The white hospital room, without shadows or corners, has become a haven for truth in several episodes ("Treason," "Mother," "Third Person"). Sean Callery's wistful soundtrack underscores a guileless admission from Michael. It is easy to see why this episode is the overwhelming Season One fan favorite. As Joel Surnow has remarked, "Dumping shit on Nikita keeps our audience interested."

Music

"Majick" by **Keoki** on *Ego-Trip* (Moonshine Records) — Nikita working out

Guest Cast

James Faulkner (Inquisitor), Costa Kamateros (Garsha)

120 VERDICT

Written by Robert Cochran
Directed by Gilbert Shilton

Section One is again called in to protect Jovan Mijovich (newly elected as leader of his country) when he becomes the target of an assassination attempt at his inaugural ball. The assassin is eliminated, but no one is prepared when a small band of rebels holds the partygoers hostage to coerce an admission of war crimes from the new premier.

Despite the above-average guest cast of David Calderisi and Eric Peterson, "Verdict" fails to capture the horrors of the play from which it draws its inspiration: Ariel Dorfman's Death and the Maiden. Kate Greenhouse is moving as Maria, a courageous woman who forgoes revenge to spare her family pain and her country another war. But the bond of torture and pain she shares with Nikita (fresh from the trials of "War") goes unexplored. Nikita's impulse to kill Mijovich seems a step backward for the character, and it minimizes her cool-headed accomplishments of the previous hour, however contrived. She has already seen Section defend monsters to protect a greater good. Well, at least the absurdity of a Section One operative guiding the course of a hostage negotiation does not go unnoticed by Mijovich, as he squirms his way through the final plea-bargaining scene.

Nikita's and Operations' curiosity about Michael's relationship with the dead contact hangs in the wind undeveloped, barely affording Michael the chance to reestablish his position as an unfeeling bastard after the tenderness of "War." In spite of the promise of the sunny teaser, humorously underscored by P.J. Harvey's "Working for the Man" (and featuring the improbable coincidence of Michael's visit to the same park as Nikita), the episode remains visually uninteresting, with the exception of the black-and-white high-contrast flashbacks and the claustrophobic vent scenes.

L — "19th Century Garden," east side of St. James Cathedral at King and Church Streets
S — Nikita spots Michael in the park

L — Gazebo in the park
(east side of St. James Cathedral)
S — Michael meets his contact

Above:
L — gates of the "Sculpted Garden" (115 King St. East, across from St. James Cathedral)
S — Nikita watches Michael and the contact

Left:
L — inside gates of the "Sculpted Garden"
S — the contact's car explodes

L — Courtyard of Casa Loma, Spadina and Davenport Roads
S — Mijovich's Embassy

Music

"Working For the Man" by **P.J. Harvey** on *To Bring You My Love* (Polygram/ Island Records) — Nikita follows Michael in the park

Guest Cast

Eric Peterson (Zoran), David Calderisi (Jovan Mijovich), Kate Greenhouse (Maria), John-Patrick Mavric (Alexei), Mary Moore (Griffin), Joanna Bacalso (Woman Friend)

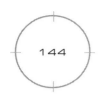
121 BRAINWASHED

Written by Peter Bellwood
Directed by René Bonnière

When a futuristic contraption called a "phasing shell" is discovered in the apartment of a suicidal suspect, Nikita is chosen to test its operation, and she discovers its therapeutic potential. The shell's efficacy as a brainwashing device is not apparent even as Nikita begins to suffer hallucinations and symptoms of addiction to its seductive powers of relief.

The performances take center stage in this episode, but there are some other notable elements. The story fills in some of the details in Nikita's back story, emphasizing episodes of victimization (she was traumatized during a childhood beating by school-yard bullies and later by her mother's abusive boyfriend). The solarized look of Nikita's hallucinations as they recede creates an effective mood. Madeline's use of the sound of Park's heartbeat as a ready-made lie detector is reminiscent of "War." (Hey, if it worked for the Inquisitor, why not Madeline?) And there is some humor from Walter, the sixties throw-back, spotting Nikita "jones-ing" for another session in the phasing shell. Michael's devotion in the face of Nikita's breakdown and assassination-suicide attempt is moving.

An inspired nod to the spy classic *The Manchurian Candidate*, "Brainwashed" is an interesting mix of high-tech and high drama. It is easy to understand why this episode is a favorite for Peta Wilson. Working with one of her favorite directors, René Bonnière, Wilson gives the rich material in Peter Bellwood's script a run for its money. She is able to convey Nikita's tailspin into addiction and a nervous breakdown through a balance of physical, emotional, and psychological expressions. Who can forget the discovery of Nikita, feet in the kitchen sink, lost to her demons? The stage is set for Nikita's crisis of faith in "Mercy," the season finale.

L — Ontario Place walkways, Harbourfront
S — Michael arrives at the phasing shell lab

Music

"Butterfly Lovers Violin Concerto" by **Chen Gang, He Zhan Hao** on *Concerto for Violin: "Butterfly Lovers"* (Marco Polo) — Nikita tries to kill the Chinese premier

Guest Cast

Janet Lo (Chan Park), William Colgate (Shadowy Man), Steve Mousseau (Reilly), David Dunbar (Tour Guide), Fred Lee (Premier Hua Feng), Alex Stapley (Young Nikita), Connor Devitt (Bully)

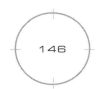
122 MERCY

Written by Michael Loceff
Directed by Joseph L. Scanlan

Stanley Shays is the Birkoff of the explosives world: a genius, innocent of the ways of the outside world, and satisfied with the pursuit of his research. But he's created an undetectable and powerful weapon, and Section One is in a race against time to prevent the formula from falling into enemy hands.

This is an episode of confessions and truths. Madeline is unexpectedly forthright when she tells Nikita that she will *never* have the freedom she seeks regardless of how well she performs. Nikita, for her part, has finally realized that what she needs cannot and should not be sought in the person of Michael, or anybody else for that matter. Michael is

L — Gooderham and Worts, south side, at Parliament Street
S — Nikita tells Michael she couldn't kill Stanley

finally honest both with Nikita, when he tells her that he's been protecting her from the start but can no longer do so, and with himself, when he gives up his need to mold her into a cold op.

"Mercy" is a dense episode that could have (and perhaps should have) been a two-parter. It is possibly the most emotional episode of Season One, with "War" running a close second. Peta Wilson's challenge is to take Nikita from the ease of the opening dance (presumably at peace with the demons that plagued her in "Brainwashed") through a suicide attempt (foiled only by Michael's fortuitous timing) to the elation of her escape from Section. She rises to it ably.

Nikita's descent into despair comes fast and hard, triggered by her refusal to kill Stanley in cold blood. But she makes a mistake: the torture and captivity he endures makes it clear his execution would have been a mercy killing. Ironically, the mercy she cannot show Stanley is the grace she receives from Michael. He saves her life twice: in the inadvertent disruption of her suicide and in the ultimate gift of her freedom.

Music

"The Love Thieves" by **Depeche Mode** on *Ultra* (Mute Records) — throughout

Guest Cast

Sean Whalen (Stanley Shays), Richard Clarkin (Tyler), Alan Mozes (Spidel), Gerry Salsberg (Tribunal Man), James Kirchner (Operative), Kay Valley (Operative #2)

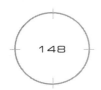

SEASON TWO

201 HARD LANDING

Written by Michael Loceff
Directed by Jon Cassar

After six months of life on the run, Nikita is captured by Freedom League agents. When she overhears a plan to ambush and massacre her old colleagues, she escapes and is reunited with Michael.

Writer Michael Loceff faces a daunting challenge in this episode: he must make Nikita's return to Section believable both for Operations and for the audience. As we have seen so often in the past, Nikita's love for Michael has been a powerful motivation, and the circumstances of her reunion with him afford the perfect cover for her return to Section. But in solving one problem the writers face the danger of creating a new one: the so-called *Moonlighting* syndrome.

This episode is remembered as the one where Nikita and Michael finally "do it." But in consummating the series' central relationship, the show risks losing that all-important sexual tension that has viewers tuning in week after week. That said, it would have been unbelievable if they had not made love, and Loceff's script ensures that the love scene is not lacking the signature elements of violence, restraint, and control that have marked the relationship thus far. Not only is the sexual act off-screen (unlike in other episodes: "Obsessed," "Double Date," "Off Profile"), but the voluntary beating Nikita takes at Michael's hands is very intimate and, ironically, almost tender. That note of sadomasochism sounds twice here. But Loceff also gives us the morning-after scene in which the lovers, bathed in light, are stripped bare; it is this scene that will stand in painful contrast to Nikita's new trials once back in Section.

L — Cherry Restaurant, 275 Cherry Street
(at Commissioners Street)
S — Where Nikita is working when the Freedom
League catches up with her

L — 275 Cherry Street, rear of the Cherry
Restaurant
S — Nikita attempts to escape her captors

L — Toronto Docks
S — "The Boat" where Nikita and Michael are reunited

The episode excels visually as well as dramatically. Production Designer Rocco Matteo's club and foreign-location sets are always fun, imaginative, and a real change of pace from the more minimalist, stark environments of Section One. The Thai club is both exotic — lit with reds, blues, and yellows — and futuristic, with its corridor of convex mirrors. Red targeting lasers add drama to the action sequences with classic *La Femme Nikita* flair: the ultra-cool Michael disables his target with one hand while continuing to nuzzle a prostitute's neck. The hour concludes with a sensual little gesture from Peta Wilson, as Nikita licks the fingers that have just been caressing Michael's chin. Unfortunately, it will be her last taste of intimacy for some time. . . .

Music

"The Love Thieves" by **Depeche Mode** on *Ultra* (Mute Records) — Michael misses Nikita

Guest Cast

Earl Pastko (Freedom League Leader), David Nerman (Ackerman), Johnie Chase (Matty)

202 SPEC OPS

Written by Robert Cochran
Directed by T.J. Scott

Michael and Nikita come under some suspicion, and Nikita is assigned a new trainer.

This three-episode arc begins with a stylish opening scene, set to the music of Prodigy. In a white-on-white room, Nikita is bored, captive, and under surveillance, pacing like a caged animal. The opening scene is typical of this episode, which is filled with astounding visuals. The Hong Kong scene is possibly the series' best chase sequence. Edited by Richard Wells and set to Orbital's "Satan," the scene is vividly lit with greens, purples, and reds and is stylishly shot by T.J. Scott. It is Michael, rather than Nikita, whom we now see wearing sunglasses, which reflect back to us his off-kilter world. Later, another amazing image of Michael — the master of masks — presents itself as he is shot through a face etched in a blacked-out window. The unearthly sound of the silencer adds to the surreal flavor of the scene. Writer Robert Cochran is giving us a man who is rapidly losing his poker face, making errors, and not even lying particularly well. Losing his trademark control (about to dishonor himself?) and afraid of more than cancellation, Michael's threatened disintegration is projected flawlessly by Dupuis.

Nikita and Michael's continued deception is a house of cards always threatening to collapse under its own weight. They meet in back corners and secret hallways, their labyrinth of lies is reflected in the physical space as they are shot through grillwork as through a cage. Paranoia is raised to a new pitch: Michael is correct when he asserts that any intimacy between them will show in their demeanors and they will be cancelled. And when he tells her to get over it, he speaks to her like the child she is becoming in the hands of the writers. An unfortunate side effect of Nikita's overt desire is that she seems bratty and whiny, a characterization that will take the writers almost half the season to get past.

Bruce Payne joins the cast as Jurgen, whose history with Michael is hinted at but not explored — a potentially exciting opportunity missed. Payne gives Jurgen a "tell": every time he takes off his glasses he's being sincere or honest. It is a variation on Nikita's use of glasses, but it's a bit heavy handed, as is the British actor's American accent. Apparently, the notion was to create a kind of Zen master spiritual guru type as a change of pace from the cold, undemonstrative Michael.

Along with some new areas of Section, like "reprogramming" with its geodesic training pod, Madeline gets a new office: harder, colder than her previous one, despite the addition of plant life. How appropriate that the plants are orchids and bonsai trees — controlled and highly cultivated. One real surprise is Madeline's comment: "A bond between two agents isn't always such a bad thing." This comment lays the foundation for a third-season shocker, and subtly introduces the second-season revelations about her shared history with Operations.

Music

"Smack My Bitch Up" by **Prodigy** from *The Fat of the Land* (Maverick/Warner Brothers) — Nikita in the observation room

"Satan (Industry Standard Mix)" by **Orbital** from *In Sides* (Internal Records) — Michael's chase in Hong Kong

Guest Cast

Bruce Payne (Jurgen), Nicu Branzea (Kudrin), Derwin Jordan (Marco)

203 THIRD PERSON

Written by Michael Loceff
Directed by Jon Cassar

Nikita's retraining is concluded, and she returns to full status. But Michael fears Jurgen's interest in Nikita may cover a desire to blackmail the former lovers.

The arc continues with Nikita and Jurgen's growing closeness. With Michael listening in on the pair — voyeurism at its height — we get an early indication that Michael has a mission to perform and that we have an hour of manipulations ahead. Jurgen expounds his Zen-like philosophies in a lecture on life outside Section and the meaning of freedom. Still, he isn't immune when Michael pushes his buttons,

L — North side of Front Street across from Union Station
S — Nikita and Jurgen have coffee

and the two come to blows. It is a rare demonstration of emotion on Michael's part. The fight operates on several levels. While on the surface it appears to be about Nikita, there is also Michael's manipulation of Jurgen's emotions when he creates a repeat scenario of the incident that landed Jurgen in Section in the first place, the challenge for alpha-male dominance (as Jurgen is outside the normal command structure), Michael's guilt about the betrayal that has begun, and a hint of some unspoken past conflict. It is both humorous and noteworthy that while the men beat on each other, Nikita blows off steam by tearing down a wall and reconstructing her apartment.

The theme of primal conflict continues as Nikita is sent by Michael to kill Jurgen. The romantic triangle that is emerging is reflected in the tripartite struggle for survival. Michael is trying to insure their political survival (how can the couple keep their secrets and stay alive without Jurgen holding some power over them?), Nikita believes they are fighting for their lives (Section will kill them if they find out Michael helped her escape) and Jurgen seems to be fighting to save Nikita's soul (his comment, "You're his slave," hits the mark and precipitates a cathartic breakthrough for Nikita). Still, how betrayed Michael must feel when he has lied and murdered to protect the two of them, and he sees Jurgen still alive.

Music

"Weird Planet" by **Headrillaz** from *Coldharbour Rocks* (BMG/V2/Gee Street General Techno) — Nikita tears down a wall in her apartment

Guest Cast

Bruce Payne (Jurgen), Michael Querin (Pontriargan)

204 APPROACHING ZERO

Written by Michael Loceff
Directed by René Bonnière

As Nikita and Jurgen grow closer, Madeline recruits Michael to acquire the information Jurgen is using to hold Operations hostage.

Nikita's apartment gets a new look this season. It is colder, more modern, less personal, and less revealing than her previous one. As Nikita grows this season and begins to fit into Section, her personal physical space begins to reflect the repression of her eccentricities. In fact, she goes so far as to bring a piece of Section home with her: the white tulip chair from the Observation Room. She is entertaining the idea of a relationship with someone from Section. Nikita's real attraction to Jurgen seems to stem from the special arrangement he has whereby he retains some control over his timetable and his life. He has a modicum of freedom within Section, and can say no to certain things. It's a power and freedom Nikita wants for herself.

It will take the writers several episodes to bring Nikita's behavior back on an even keel. For now, her "maybe, maybe not" attitude is childish and her hope that Michael is jealous is repellant. After the conflicts of "Third Person," her physical shyness with Michael as he pretends to pull off the transmitter is believable, and speaks to the cost of their failed conspiracy to exclude Jurgen from their secrets.

Dupuis is marvelous as Michael listens in on Nikita and Jurgen's initial stages of lovemaking. Madeline at least has the discretion to leave him to his barely disguised humiliation. Michael later uses Nikita again to achieve another objective: in this case to secure access to Jurgen's house and thereby destroy the intel Jurgen is using to hold Operations ransom (again proving that Section is not as invincible as it portrays itself). Caught in the middle, Michael maintains his loyalty to Section, but the urgency with which he prevents Nikita and Jurgen

L — St. Leonard Hotel (418 Sherbourne Street)
S — Nikita and Jurgen collect the shooter

from having sex indicates a jealousy of Nikita, and also shows that he is fighting to protect her within the political system that controls them both. It is a tension that will begin to wear Michael down over the course of the series.

Peta Wilson and Roy Dupuis are terrific in the pivotal scene — their face-off in Section — where each offers a silent, barely detectable gesture of assent to a private discussion. The exchange is as revealing of their connection as if they had continued to sleep together. The change in Nikita is visible in her level of control and her adoption of acceptable Section behavior. In the category of "too little, too late" come Michael's revelations that he keeps his feelings separate from the job, living his life as a person split in two. His final confession, that he lied to further the case against Jurgen, may rank as Michael's first indisputably guileless admission. Unfortunately, the emotional implications inherent in killing off his mentor — a father figure of sorts — are left unexplored.

Music

"Burn" by **Sister Machine Gun** from *Burn* (TVT Records) — search of the ship

"Carrouella" by **Les Jumeaux** from *Feathercut* (ITN Corp) — attempt to stop the computer upload

Guest Cast

Bruce Payne (Jurgen), Farzad Sadrian (Arka)

205 NEW REGIME

Written by Robert Cochran
Directed by Jon Cassar

Petrosian returns and steps in as leader of Section when Operations is shot by a Section operative. Nikita is chosen as his second-in-command, but learns that power comes with a price.

The truly shocking image of Operations gunned down in the middle of a briefing opens this age-old tale of a struggle for power. Nikita's lesson is a harsh one as she spies, lies, bullies, and almost kills in cold blood. Thinking there might be freedom with the power she has seen others wield, she agrees to act as Petrosian's second-in-command (Nigel Bennett reprises his role from "Rescue"). What follows is a

L — Osgoode Hall (Queen Street and University Avenue)
S — Michael's mission to collect the disk

continuation of a tone set at the beginning of this season. Nikita's worst characteristics come to the fore — she is smarmy, smug, self-satisfied, and arrogant. Tarted up with bright red lips and big hair, she looks like a spoiled child who has gotten into Mommy's makeup bag. Mercifully, it marks the lowest point in Nikita's tour of the other side and the writers start to pull her back on track in the next episode.

Nikita's foray into the Section power structure is one of a series of firsts in this episode, which also includes the first on-screen cancellation, performed with film-noir flair by Madeline, and our first hint at the depth of Madeline and Operations' history and connection. She wills him to live, and Alberta Watson is great to watch as she orders the doctors to save his life. Operations' shooting, all the more startling for not being a Section contrivance designed to flush out an enemy, serves to expose cracks in Section's seemingly impenetrable political and power structure. In the end, this is Nikita's most valuable lesson.

Music

"Do What You Have To Do" by **Sarah McLachlan** from *Surfacing* (Arista, Nettwerk Records) — Nikita meets Michael in the bar

"Path to the Invisible" by **Pilgrimage** from *9 Songs of Ecstasy* (Point Music) — Michael searches for the CD

Guest Cast

Nigel Bennett (Petrosian), Dean McDermott (Sikes)

206 MANDATORY REFUSAL

Written by David Ehrman
Directed by Ken Girotti

When his communications are manipulated by an enemy, Michael adopts a protocol known as "mandatory refusal," whereby he will ignore all communications with Section until his original mission is complete. Unbeknownst to him, his target is holding Madeline prisoner to insure his safe passage out of the country.

"Mandatory Refusal" is the story of two couples, each trying to save their respective partners and breaking the rules to do it. Operations, fresh from his near-death experience of "New Regime," shows signs of tenderness toward Madeline that concern her rather than please her. As it turns out, she has every reason to be worried, for when she is kidnapped (how did *that* happen?) the rule book goes out the window. Glazer is wonderful as the inconsolable Operations, and Watson beautifully portrays Madeline, whose courage in the face of torture is astounding. Not only does she issue corrective instructions to her torturer on how to use the equipment, but she exhibits the physical control to rival her psychological and emotional control when she consciously stops *and restarts* her own heart! The incident helps build the character's mythology.

Michael, too, exhibits near superhuman prowess when he fends off the attack of his peers, shaking off the effects of a tranquilizer dart and remaining one step ahead of all of Operations' resources. Only Nikita comes close to catching up with him. Like Operations, she acts autonomously, effecting Madeline's rescue and consequently saving Michael's life. Unfortunately, the parallels don't end here: the dynamics of the relationships reveal the hard realities of life inside Section. While Nikita and Operations are just happy to have their other half safe, Madeline and Michael only see the threat to stability. Michael delivers the cruelest blow of all when he tells Nikita he cannot allow her to become his "weakness." It is a central emotional question of the series: does strength lie in ruthlessness or in compassion?

Music

"Skin Against Skin" by DJ **Krush featuring Deborah Anderson** from *Milight* (Polygram Records) — Michael on his way to meet Enquist

"Chinese Burn" by **Curve** from *Chinese Burn* (Universal Records) — Michael gets shot by tranquilizer dart

Guest Cast

Gregory Hlady (Dorian Enquist), Roman Podhara (Mowen), Christopher Clements (Stillman), Chantal Quesnel (Sonia)

207 DARKNESS VISIBLE

Written by David Ehrman
Directed by Ken Girotti

Nikita and Michael are sent to the Balkans to stop an arms buyer named Luca, but the mission becomes complicated when they rescue a pair of children.

In spite of some intriguing scenes and shifting character dynamics, this episode, ripped from the headlines, fails to hit the mark. It may be, as Surnow suggests, that the hour is ambitiously production-heavy, or that the sympathy we are supposed to feel for the children is never fully realized. It may be simply too topical in theme. Even the secondary Birkoff–Gail story line, as intriguing as it is, seems to be filler that might have been better employed in another episode.

Nonetheless, it is refreshing to see Nikita's approach with Michael beginning to change. Instead of arguing with him or convincing Michael of their responsibilities, she speaks her mind and leaves it to him to play the bad guy. Yet, over the course of the episode, *he* becomes the voice of moral outrage and personal sympathy. He returns to pick up the children rather than leave them to fend for themselves at a refugee camp. Unmoved by Luca's strategic pleas for his life, Michael executes him. It is Michael who suggests they find the children's parents and who counsels the boy not to look back as they leave the parents behind. It goes a long way to humanizing a man who often appears entirely devoid of any human emotion.

Birkoff's disturbing decision to turn in his first love, when he discovers Gail has been using Section intel to steal money, might have seemed a more significant event in another episode. As it is, his moral dilemma turns out to be just a test of his middle-management skills, courtesy of Madeline.

La Femme Nikita's open endings are one of its great attractions, and this episode is no exception. Writer David Ehrman cleverly plays against our expectations with the closing tag, in which we see the children and their parents reunited. When the reunion turns out to be Nikita's dream it is less a cheat than it is evidence of her compassion and guilt burrowing into her subconscious.

Music

Original music by Sean Callery

Guest Cast

Kyle Downes (Peter), Kevi Katsuras (Sasha), Tara Slone (Gail), Damir Andrei (Cain), Ned Vukovich (Luca), Anna-Louis Richardson (Anna), Andy Rukavina (Gregory)

208 HALF LIFE

Written by Maurice Hurley
Directed by René Bonnière

While attempting to defuse a bomb, Michael recognizes the handiwork of an old colleague from his pre-Section days. Madeline and Operations seize the opportunity and send Michael to execute his former mentor, René Dian.

Once again a Section recruit turns out to be more human than monstrous, and not the cold-blooded killer we've come to expect. And it is quite shocking to learn that political protest once motivated Michael's behavior and that he fought for a cause.

Nikita and Michael experience something of a role reversal here. Nikita initially deceives Section to protect Michael. Later, in a refreshing shift of power, she proceeds with the mission to capture Dian, admonishing Michael the way he has done to her in the past. Nikita's instincts are improving — she suspects a deeper and more personal motive behind Michael's deceptions. She has also become much

L — Union Station
S — Michael locates René Dian

L — Bright Street
S — Michael watches his sister and her family

L — Bright Street
S — Michael parks the car near his sister's
house

L — 264 The Esplanade
S — Nikita's apartment

Right:

L — Cloud Gardens, Temperance Street
S — Michael discovers René's bomb and Nikita
evacuates the area

more adept at playing the Section game, spying on Michael (with some of the coolest surveillance equipment to date) and using Birkoff to pass on her intel. (A humorous moment occurs when an impatient Nikita deflates Birkoff's evident pleasure with the progress he's making in his search for Dian by delivering the bomber's location and tracker frequency.)

As the writers fill in the blanks of the characters' lives, there is always a risk that in humanizing them they will diminish their power or mystique. The potential for such a disaster is present as we learn of Michael's history as a student in the Paris University riots of 1984. But Maurice Hurley's script, directed by the incomparable René Bonnière, is a complex examination of regret and disillusionment, of loyalty and friendship. The confluence of Michael's past with his present drives him to a dangerous self-examination. By the episode's climax he is willing to submit to René's judgment that along with his beliefs, he has lost his soul. René's death is not meaningless, and Michael unexpectedly derives three gifts from it. He observes his sister (whom René raised as his own) in person, albeit at a distance; he gains a new perspective on an old enemy as his sister and her loving family are the very bourgeois he once sought to destroy; he redefines his relationship with Nikita by giving her the gift of his past and his trust in their most intimate exchange to date.

Music

"Tangent" by **Beth Orton** from *Trailer Park* (Heavenly Records) — Nikita is following Michael

"Les Bourgeois" by **Jacques Brel** — René sings to Michael

Guest Cast

Denis Forest (René), Genevieve Langlois (Jeanine), Martine Rochon (Michael's sister)

209 FIRST MISSION

Written by Peter Mohan & Jim Henshaw
Directed by Guy Magar

Nikita is promoted to team leader a full three years ahead of the standard training schedule. When one member of her team proves difficult to control, Nikita struggles to reconcile her unconventional approach with the mission objectives.

When all hell breaks loose at Section and Nikita is promoted, the impression is that she is on Section's fast track. (The writers drop an intriguing hint about Michael's early promotion through the ranks, and one wonders just what was so different in his case.) There is also the suggestion that Nikita is getting a taste of her own medicine in having to deal with a rebellious operative like herself. Between her how-to-handle-difficult-people lessons from Michael and Operations stacking the deck by designing the last mission to eliminate Vizcano, Nikita finds herself incorporating more and more of Section's methodology into her own.

Vizcano's jealousy of Michael seems contrived. The exchange between Vizcano and Nikita is maudlin and belittles her earlier characterization as a bitch with attitude. As the unstable, jilted lover-wannabe, her observations about Michael's need for a quest are unreliable and irrelevant. Happily, her observation that Section wants their recruits to "imprint someone like an animal" has enough of the ring of truth about it to be insightful, and is a plausible explanation for Madeline's early pressure to keep Nikita and Michael in each other's thoughts.

As Nikita becomes drawn into the very world she once despised, the writers are striving to establish the delicate balance she is beginning to make between a life within Section and a life ruled by the heart. The changes are evidenced in her confrontation with Operations. They argue the nature of service to a greater good. Where Operations is focused entirely on the destination, Nikita questions the value of a journey without feeling, compassion, or hope. She argues fearlessly, even walking out on him mid-discussion. It is an early indication that she will be prepared to keep the promise Adrian will extract by the season's finale.

Music

Original music by Sean Callery

Guest Cast

Janet Kidder (Vizcano), Diego Chambers (Stark), Peter Mensah (Taylor), Neno Vojionovic (Mentz), Will Corno (Prager)

210 OPEN HEART

Written by Elliot Stern
Directed by René Bonnière

Nikita goes undercover in a women's prison to retrieve the one witness who might identify a "human bomb" on a suicide mission.

Well, they had to do it eventually: a chicks-in-prison episode! Peta Wilson has fun with the tough-girl action scenes, getting in a few head kicks, killing a guard, and kicking out a wall. Along with guest star Gina Torres and director René Bonnière, Wilson keeps the intimate scenes tender but sexually charged. But poor Nikita: even when she's making it with a girl, violence and abuse partner with sex, as the beating Nikita gets from the guards affords Jenna the opportunity to get close. Just in case the audience misses the salacious point of the make-out scene in the prison, we get the psychologically intimate equivalent in the interrogation room (for the titillation of Section's

WHERE'S WALDO?

When Joel Surnow conceived of a "mystery" with which to tease fans of the show, he never dreamed how strange the theories exchanged over the Internet would get. Rather than reveal to the audience that Nikita was "the illegitimate love child of Operations" — not — Surnow offered up clues to Season Two's two-part finale. A breadcrumb trail of appearances by "Goatee Man" (played by property masters Jim and Geoff Murrin) was the treat left for the observant fan or devotee with a VCR. For those of you who missed "Goatee Man's" (and sometimes, "Men's") appearances, here is a checklist:

Episode #	Episode Name	Appearance
205	New Regime	Goatee Man is seated at a table in the restaurant where Michael is sent to meet Nikita
207	Half Life	Goatee Man is evacuated from the park in the opening scene
211	Psychic Pilgrim	Goatee Man is walking his dog as Michael leaves the house
212	Soul Sacrifice	Goatee Man in a beret observes Nikita watching Michael exiting Terry's apartment
214	Old Habits	Goatee Man is seated at the bar in the club where Nikita meets Formitz for the first time
216	Not Was	Goatee Man is waiting outside Perez's club; Goatee twins exchange papers inside the club's front lobby
217	Double Date	Goatee Man is inside the cyber-café where Birkoff is playing video games
218	Off Profile	Goatee Man is at the party where Nikita observes Michael and Andrea dancing
219	Last Night	Goatee twins play chess in the park while Nikita chases Julia into the pipe
220	In Between	Goatee Man arrives at Nikita's apartment, introduced as "Steven," Carla's boyfriend; Goatee Man takes Carla's phone call in the final scene
221	Adrian's Garden	Goatee Man assures Adrian over the phone that the plane she hears was a diverted commercial flight
222	End Game	Goatee twins lie dead in Adrian's house, having been executed by Section One

male population). Operations is amused, and Birkoff's jaw drops ever so slightly; at least Michael (more conscious of the price Nikita is paying) has the grace to look uncomfortable as Jenna's accusation that Nikita is a whore hits its mark.

You have to love Red Cell, though; they come up with the most ingenious plans to destroy Section. This time it's a bomb with a "bio-trigger," planted in the woman who is supposed to be a witness to the operation that placed the bomb in a man. Knowing full well operatives will bring their prisoner back to Section, Red Cell sits and waits for Section to become the unwitting accomplices in their own demise. Elliot Stern's clever premise has an equally inventive resolution as Michael, ever the shrewd strategist, deduces it is Jenna's reflection that holds the truth of the bomber's identity. It is brilliant in its simplicity. And after all is said and done, it's business as usual in Section. The thud of Jenna's explosion doesn't even interrupt the comings and goings of Section life.

Music

Original music by Sean Callery

Guest Cast

Gina Torres (Jenna Vogler), Jill Dyck (Belinda), David Collins (Dr. Kerlock), Vince Guerriero (Stanko), Alice Poon (Adrian)

211 PSYCHIC PILGRIM

Written by Michael Loceff
Directed by René Bonnière

Nikita goes undercover as a psychic in hopes of luring a terrorist into the open.

Writer Michael Loceff puts the tease in teaser this time around. The opening scene is any fan's wet dream as we encounter Nikita and Michael, in apparent domestic bliss, snuggling in bed. But we can't be fooled that easily!

René Bonnière and Peta Wilson take what could easily have been a cheesy sentimental setup and, with guest star Joaqim de Almeida, create the very moving scenes of a father in anguish seeking the forgiveness of his dead young son. But this episode is less about the mission than the effects of being undercover, not just for Nikita but for the normally impassive Michael. In fact, there are hints that Michael enjoyed playing house on this mission. He requests Nikita as his partner and is fairly artless at disguising his motives when she asks him about the choice. Loceff, refreshingly, offers none of the usual lectures from Madeline on the emotional risks of such a mission. Instead, Madeline issues Nikita some cold instructions on the sexual behavior of newlyweds. The result is an oddly embarrassing, rather than titillating, love scene. In the brilliant morning-after scene, Michael seems to be talking in code, and Wilson and Dupuis create a personal and moving moment as the two "lovers" fumble to reach each other in their performance for the surveillance cameras. Paired with the final scene (in which Michael offers the priceless gift of hope to Nikita), it is some of their best work together.

In a parallel tale of parent-child forgiveness, Madeline seeks redemption from her dying mother in the death of her sister, Sarah. It is not surprising that she has built her identity on that one event, nor is it unreasonable for her to hope that her perceptions as a child might have been inaccurate and that the blame and responsibility she took on was self-inflicted. She finds no solace, in spite of Operations' gift of the visit to see her mother (defying all Section protocols). These revelations bring insights into Madeline's motivations and prepare the way for the merciless and psychologically loaded decisions of "End Game."

Music

Original music by Sean Callery

Guest Cast

Joaquim de Almeida (Armel), Susan Kottmann (Faye), Marcus Spilotro (Louis), Christopher Clements (Stillman), David Gayle (Tonio)

212 SOUL SACRIFICE

Written by Michael Loceff
Directed by David Warry-Smith

Nikita finds a new friend in Terry, a longtime Section One operative. When she learns of Terry's pregnancy she is determined to help her colleague protect the unborn child.

To this point Nikita's relationships with other women have been warm, intriguing, or compelling. Unfortunately, this time nothing really gels for either the story or the actors. Years of service in Section have hardened Terry, and it shows; it's hard to suddenly warm to the woman just because she is pregnant. Still, the premise is intriguing: what *does* happen to pregnant operatives and their children? As Terry observes, there is no day care in Section.

Nikita is getting better at lying and is developing a better sense of when to trust Michael. It pays off here as Michael covers for Terry

ve:
— Scott Street and Colborne
— "Le Grand Hotel"

Right:
L — Leader Street
S — Goatee Man watches Nikita

Above:
L — Front Street, South Side, near Leader Street
S — Michael and Terry leave her apartment

Left:
L — Colborne and Leader Streets
S — Nikita observes Michael and Terry

when she tries to run and arranges for an abortion if Terry wants to keep Section ignorant of her predicament. Unfortunately, Michael's compassion exposes Terry to manipulation by an enemy and gets Michael shot, calling into question the choices Nikita so frequently advocates.

There are some lighter moments in this generally overwrought episode. Carlo Rota returns as a cartoonish version of Mick Schtoppel. His endless shtick provides some comic relief and a great pay-off when Michael throws him out of a moving limousine. Wilson provides a cute moment at the party while Nikita plays the bubble-headed blond and teases Michael with a couple of dance moves intended for his eyes. The real humor lies in Walter's absurdly hilarious three-year review. Subjected to a series of inane questions for which there cannot possibly be right answers, Don Francks takes the cranky Walter through his paces as a highly amused Operations looks on. What could possibly be the question for which "eyeball" is the correct answer?

Music

"Komit" by **Juno Reactor** from *Bible of Dreams* (Wax Trax/TVT)
— Nikita and Terry in the club

Guest Cast

Khandi Alexander (Terry), Carlo Rota (Schtoppel), John Ralston (Sullivan Bates), Jason Noel (Snow)

213 FUZZY LOGIC

Written by Michael Loceff
Directed by Ken Girotti

When Birkoff is unable to crack the code used by a terrorist group breaking into a Department of Defense satellite, Section kidnaps a boy genius to do the job.

Matthew Ferguson stretches his comic muscles in this episode as Birkoff knocks heads with Gregory Hillinger, a younger, smarter version of himself. With his dry, cynical delivery, Ferguson gives the hour a particular tone and appeal. There are several points of comparison between the two prodigies. Birkoff's intolerance of his colleagues in the opening scene is echoed in Gregory's treatment of Birkoff, and there is a suggestive silence when Gregory asks Birkoff if he was kidnapped, too.

Nikita's incident with her new neighbor Barry and his drug-dealing pals means little apart from her ease in dealing with a problem and working within Section rules to effect a cleanup. However, her tough-love tour for Gregory of Section's torture chamber is a timely reminder that Section isn't all cooperation, compromise, and reason. As Nikita has worked her way through the ranks and Madeline and Operations have become more humanized, it can be easy to forget just how barbaric her overseers really are. The shocking scene of an operative being tortured for going out on a date with an old girl-friend resensitizes the audience to the potential perils of making mistakes within Section and suggests that Nikita is no longer fighting every injustice, but rather picking her fights more carefully. When Section tricks Hillinger in the climax, it is Nikita, disguised as the boy's mother, who has perpetrated the deceit.

Music

Original music by Sean Callery

Guest Cast

Kris Lemche (Greg Hillinger), Dan Redican (Barry), Eva Crawford (Rita)

214 OLD HABITS

Written by Maurice Hurley
Directed by Terry Ingram

Nikita discovers her contact with Bright Star is actually a psychotic serial killer, whom Section is protecting.

Chris Leavins is wonderful as the cold, dead-eyed, sniggering psycho killer Formitz. And Section is up to its old tricks, protecting a sociopath in hopes of saving many lives from a series of suicide bombings. It is a classic *La Femme Nikita* dilemma. Does Nikita protect one life or many, and does Section's sanctioning of criminal behavior create even bigger monsters? Nikita has come a long way since Season One, and it is intriguing that she is able to control her rage, which once might have caused her to kill the man outright rather than beat him senseless. Truth is in short supply as Nikita and Michael play a round of who's lying to whom; this time Nikita wins when she leaks Formitz's betrayal of Bright Star and allows them to take care of his execution. It is a clever solution, perfectly in keeping with Section mind games. It's even a little unnerving that she does it so well. Wilson closes the scene with a lovely little I-wash-my-hands-of-it gesture as she flicks away the memory of the bug that was Formitz.

There is no justice on the personal front within Section, either. The little time Birkoff was able to give Walter and his new love,

L — Metro Hall, 55 John Street
S — Nikita and Michael look for the bomber

Inset:
L — Wellington Street near John Street
S — The "bus stop" explodes

Below:
L — Sunnyside Pavilion
S — The market

L — Sunnyside Pavilion (Lakeshore Boulevard West)
S — Fomitz enters the market

L — Sunnyside Pavilion
S — Fomitz moves through the market

L — Sunnyside Pavilion
S — Michael captures Halir

Belinda, has now expired. Francks, Ferguson, and Wilson do a great job with Walter's crisis when he learns that his wife has been killed as an abeyance operative on a mission. Ready for revenge, Walter is consoled by Nikita but is soon face-to-face with Operations and barely able to contain himself. It's a tension-filled scene that works beautifully.

Music

"(Can't You Trip) Like I Do" by **Filter/The Crystal Method** from *Spawn Soundtrack* (Vegas Sony Music) — chasing the suicidal bomber

"Space" by **Keoki** from *Altered Egotrip* (Moonshine) — Nikita pulls Formitz off Danielle in the bar

Guest Cast

Chris Leavins (Gregory Formitz), Donna Christo (Danielle), Cas Anvar (Halir), Eric Fink (Amar), T.L. Fursberg (Erica), Jill Dyck (Belinda), Stavroula Logothettis (Kara)

215 INSIDE OUT

Written by Maurice Hurley
Directed by Ken Girotti

When a lethal variant of the anthrax virus begins to spread within Section, Nikita and Michael may be the only hope for the people trapped inside.

Red Cell is at it again. In yet another creative attempt to bring down their enemies, they lead Section One to an abandoned laboratory, knowing that operatives will return with samples of the materials they find on-site. So begins a rather claustrophobic hour during which Section becomes something of a pressure cooker. This is a character-driven episode, but the real hero inside Section is Birkoff who, having just been dumped by Gail, remains level-headed throughout — even under the threat of cancellation from an irate Operations.

Eugene Robert Glazer has some real fun right from the get go. Even before the threat, disunity is evident as Operations breaks into one of Madeline's interrogations, undermines her authority by questioning her priorities, and executes her prisoner on the spot. It's a startling and uncharacteristic moment that carries into the passageway and under the gaze of Nikita. The question of whether Madeline and Operations are lovers will be played out to the end of Season Three. But before then, we get an intriguing glimpse into the pair's history when Madeline succumbs to the virus and Operations breaks every procedural and physical barrier to be with her. Watson and Glazer are always a treat to watch, and the scene mirrors Madeline's confrontation with the doctors in "New Regime."

The real shock of the episode, though, is the realization that Madeline's brush with death hasn't softened her in the least as she orders a personnel review in the wake of the panic and emotion of the previous day. She may be acting out against Operations' behavior, or she may just be retrenching as the most ruthless bitch in town.

Music

Original music by Sean Callery

Guest Cast

Paul Miller (Jenklo), Martin Doyle (Bisaroff), Tara Slone (Gail), Roman Podhara (Mowen), Joe Ross (Andy), Susan Hamann (Olga)

216 NOT WAS

Written by Michael Loceff
Directed by René Bonnière

Michael is taken prisoner during a mission and given memory-altering drugs during his interrogation. When Nikita effects his rescue she discovers that all traces of his usual personality have been removed along with his memories.

What could have been an extremely cheesy episode about Michael losing his memory becomes a rather moving exploration of the theme of identity and a commentary on the Section status quo. Inventive writing and sensitive direction make "Not Was" a fan favorite. Tantalizing and frustrating at the same time, we get an hour with an emotionally vulnerable Michael, knowing full well his only hope of survival is to regain his memory and return to his old self. This raises an interesting question about personality: how much of a person's identity is determined by experience?

If we accept that with his memories stripped away we see his true self, Michael's amnesia affords us a glimpse not only of his love for Nikita, but also of the enormous price he has paid for being treated like a caged animal. The amnesia also presents the opportunity for comment on the baffling jargon used in Section and on the cruelty of a life without family or friends. Michael gets to relive the horror of his first kill and experience the common nightmare of the fear of being discovered to be a fraud. Roy Dupuis's performance is marvelous as he takes Michael through terror, confusion, loss, love, and humor. Even before the drugs take effect and the amnesia sets in there is cause to admire Michael. His resistance to the interrogation procedure is astounding, and his courage finds its twin in Nikita, who resists his declarations of love and, to save his life, returns his memories, thus losing his "true" self.

The hour is not all melodrama, though. It's Man vs. Machine as a

Left:
L — Old Mill Restaurant,
    Old Mill Road
S — Michael enters the club

Below:
L — Old Mill Restaurant
S — Perez's club

jealous and flustered Operations fights with his keyboard attempting to check out the competition for Madeline's attentions. The opening sequence in the Latin dance club begins with a teasing and suggestive moment as Michael takes Nikita's hand down, down, down to his waistline where she finds . . . a gun. In a startling scene that could be straight out of *The X-Files*, recent abductees of Perez (the Red Cell tactician) are stored alive, naked, and hairless in glass-doored cabinets. In the rush to save Michael, no one is seen collecting these poor schmucks. And Section politics rears its ugly head again as Madeline and Operations choose to let Nikita and Michael think Michael's amnesia has gone unnoticed. It seems strange to see them hand over even the illusion of power, but the question of who is fooling whom will return with a vengeance over the next few episodes.

Music

Salsa music by **Oyeme Israel** from *Salsa Mundo* (Candela) — Nikita collects disk while dancing

"Fire and Roses" by **Mimi (Goese)** from *Soak* (WEA/Warner Brothers) — Michael hides in Nikita's apartment

Guest Cast

Sam Moses (Orlando Perez), Jonathan Cuthill (Russell), Jean Yoon (Ying Kam), Frank Bishun (Frank), Natalie Persad (Natalie)

217 DOUBLE DATE

Written by Robert Cochran
Directed by Jon Cassar

Nikita and Michael are sent on a mission with David Fanning, the criminal Nikita beat to a pulp and whose wife, Lisa, Michael seduced. Fanning, seeking revenge, holds Nikita hostage and sends Michael to retrieve his estranged wife.

Robert Cochran resurrects David Fanning, one of the more memorable villains from the first season, and Fanning's return is another one of those nasty little surprises Section enjoys springing on Nikita. Douglas O'Keeffe is powerful as the psychotic hit man and savage wife beater and plays him with glee. Jon Cassar's camera work adds to his power, especially in the opening sequence, where Fanning is shot in the foreground or from a low angle to make him appear larger than life.

It is no big surprise that Fanning is out for revenge, but that he has been able to pass Section's psychological screenings is a little hard to believe, particularly as he taunts Michael the first chance he gets with the little tidbits he's picked up in the Section rumor mill. He's a twisted soul who really gets off on the violence, the game, and the challenge Nikita presents. Just to prove it, he rewards Nikita for her attack by feeding her.

Lisa, the woman scorned in this scenario, has done some maturing after the trials of her betrayal and a life on the run. After taking whatever pleasure she might from Michael, she has him beaten. Michael, for his part, submits to the beating, hoping to turn it to his advantage (and, one imagines, partially because he deserves it). Is that regret or resignation on his face as he drugs and abducts Lisa? About to make a killer out of her, he gives her the vial containing the poisonous isotope, her "way out," but one feels a momentary chill at the possible double meaning: is it a weapon or a means of suicide?

We rarely see Michael and Birkoff together, so the scene in the cyber café is enjoyable on several levels. Cochran has written a deadly serious scene but placed it in a charming setting designed to evoke incidental humor. Birkoff's off-hour escape to play mindlessly violent computer games is a kick, and so, too, is his prowess on the low-tech PC. His back may be against the wall, but it is a monumental leap of faith for Michael to trust Birkoff to cover for him and Nikita with Operations. Birkoff blossoms under the responsibility. Of course, there is the small point of Michael's threat!

The last two scenes seem oddly out of order, and the episode drifts to an end. The issue of fooling Operations and getting away with it closes out the show, and the question of office politics remains in the fore, laying the groundwork for the rest of the season.

Music

"#1 Crush" by **Garbage** from *Romeo and Juliet Soundtrack* (Capitol Records/Alamo) — Nikita encounters Fanning in Section

"Take California" by **Propellerheads** from *Decksandrumsandrockandroll* (Grand Royal) — Birkoff in the cyber café

"Life in Mono" by **Mono** from *Formica Blues* (PGD/Polygram) — Michael meets with Lisa

"Absurd" by **Fluke** from *Risotto* (Astralwerks) — chase in the forest

Guest Cast

Douglas O'Keeffe (David Fanning), Yvonne Scio (Lisa Fanning), Reuben Thompson (Heyman), Michael Chan (Glik)

218 OFF PROFILE

Written by David Ehrman
Directed by John Fawcett

Michael's romance with the new Section profiler could have lethal consequences.

The producers take a chance sending Michael out to generate another woman scorned so soon after "Double Date," but this is a solid episode, beautifully shot and well acted. It really is fun to watch Michael lock horns with his apparent female counterpart. Actress Celine Bonnier, Roy Dupuis' real-life girlfriend, does a marvelous job creating Andrea, the latest Section over-achiever, a brittle perfectionist who is wound spring tight.

The episode is rife with Section politics as Operations and Madeline scramble to get Walter on side in the cover-up of Section's use of a forbidden protocol. Operations exhibits some degree of loyalty, refusing to cancel Walter to avoid embarrassment. Madeline hits a new unsavory low, designing a holographic image of Walter's dead wife, Belinda, and Walter's rage is understandable in the face of such an emotionally pornographic abuse of his private life.

Writer David Ehrman has also written one of the more clever and suspenseful mission sequences of the season. The action is superb, set to "Loaded Gun" by Hednoize. The notion of a heartbeat security key is highly inventive, with just the right touch of sci-fi about it, and irony abounds as Nikita scrambles to find a live technician amongst the bodies of the lab workers they have just slaughtered.

Nikita has come a long way from the bratty woman of this season's first five episodes. Her counsel to Walter and her efforts to explain Michael's history to Andrea spring from a hard-won understanding. Even Madeline can't push her buttons when she observes and applauds the growing relationship between Michael and Andrea. Madeline's grip is slipping on several fronts; she frankly admits she has no idea what makes Walter tick. Even the tantalizing answers to his three-year evaluation fail to illuminate his motivations.

Music

"Angel" by **Massive Attack** from *Mezzanine* (Virgin Records/Circa Records) — party scene

"Loaded Gun" by **Hednoize** from *La Femme Nikita Soundtrack* (TVT) — destroying the lab

"Fear and Love" by **Morcheeba** from *Big Calm* (Discovery Records) — love scene

Guest Cast

Celine Bonnier (Andrea), Jill Dyck (Belinda), Rene Beau Dean (Korda)

219 LAST NIGHT

Written by Robert Cochran
Directed by Clark Johnson

Madeline matches wits with a super-computer, while Nikita tries to determine the fate of a young girl who may have been killed in mission cross-fire.

Clark Johnson joins the roster of guest directors as he tries to extract some relevance from Robert Cochran's strangely uneven script. The two main storylines (the capture of Brutus, the HAL-inspired super-computer, and Nikita's search for a young girl) never seem to go anywhere. Nikita's quest fits the producers' mandate for a return to

L — Ontario Place
S — Brutus's Lair

Inset: Ontario Place Cinesphere

the story-telling style of Season One, but in the end there is no story. The girl, Julia, is alive, Nikita is captured, she escapes. Big surprise. Madeline philosophizes on the meaning of logic, reason, and intuition, but in the end the computer poses no lasting threat to Section *per se* and is dismantled, so who cares?

What we do get are metaphors. Brutus, the slayer of Julius Caesar, becomes a new image for Michael, Operations' heir-apparent. When the foreplay between Madeline and Operations culminates in a little hookie and nookie in "The Tower," Michael seizes the opportunity to nurse his ambition and exercise some initiative. Averting a disaster with only seconds to spare, he is censured by Operations. What follows is a skillfully written game of check and mate, as Michael and Operations, shot almost entirely in profile (like the heads on a Roman coin?), redraw the map of the kingdom. Although it too is well acted and beautifully shot in close-up, Nikita and Michael's similar "chess match" over the fate of Julia's family simply revisits old conflicts.

Still, the action sequence at the dome is great. The special effects are convincing and the action is inventive (particularly when "Blue team" rises silently out of the water and takes out the guards) and Nikita comes to the fore with a spectacular leap from the exploding geodesic dome.

Music

"Silicone" by **Mono** from *Formica Blues* (PGD Polygram) — Nikita searches for the little girl

"Gentle Rain" by **Diana Krall** from *Love Scenes* (Impulse) — Madeline and Operations in the tower

Guest Cast

Colm Feore (Voice of Brutus), Geza Kovacs (Father), Sarah Gadon (Julia), Joan Heney (Rosa), Cliff Saunders (Beeka)

220 IN BETWEEN

Written by Michael Loceff
Directed by J. Scanlon

While posing as a money launderer with Michael, Nikita is approached by a terrorist's right-hand man who claims to be a Section operative long thought dead.

Nikita is caught between Operations and Madeline in one of the best episodes of the series. The ever classy Stephen Berkoff guest stars as Charles Sand, Madeline's long lost husband. Believing Sand died nine years earlier, Madeline is at first unaware that Operations is responsible for his disappearance and subsequent inability to contact Section. But it speaks to the powerful alliances within Section's political structure that she eventually closes ranks, sides with Operations, and executes her own husband.

Nikita's attempt to hold the separate confidences of her two superiors makes for a significant change in her relationship with Michael. She has to lie to him and gets an upgrade in her status (to a class-two operative) causing a crucial shift in their mentor-protégé relationship. "You'll have to stop coming to me," he tells her as he advises her to think through her dilemma. Nikita is ready for this transition even if Michael is not (as subsequent events will show).

Alan Peterson has great fun as Abel Gelner, an ex-Red Cell agent who enjoys setting Nikita and Michael against one another almost as much as Operations does. Anais Gronofsky's welcome return as Carla presents the single most unexpected plot twist to date.

Music

"Refractions in the Plastic Pulse" by **Stereolab** from *Dots and Loops* (Elektra) — Nikita at home

"Superheros" by **Esthero** from *Breath From Another* (Sony) — Nikita has dinner with Carla and "Goatee Man"/Steven

Guest Cast

Anais Granofsky (Carla), Stephen Berkoff (Carlo Giraldi/Charles Sand), Alan Peterson (Abel Gelner), Damon D'Oliveira (Sarris), Geoff Murrin (Steven), Barna Moricz (Ellis)

221 ADRIAN'S GARDEN

Written by Michael Loceff
Directed by Brad Turner

Nikita is kidnapped by Adrian, the founder and former head of Section One. When she learns the history of Section and Operations' darker purposes, she agrees to help Adrian destroy Section.

This season ends with a beautifully written, directed, and performed two-part finale. Revelations unfold so quickly it is hard to keep up and the breathless pace is maintained to the final scene. Nikita begins her Alice-down-the-rabbit-hole journey when Carla kidnaps her and takes her to meet Adrian. The incomparable Siân Phillips guest stars as Section's creator. Her presence echoes her portrayal of the ruthless matriarch, Livia, of I, *Claudius* and that series' stories of political dirty-dealings and power games (her connection to Joel Surnow dates back to their work on his series *Covington Cross*).

The revelations begin with the removal of a "clock" (a tracking device) from Nikita's body that has been implanted by Section without her knowledge. The fact that they have been able to perpetrate such an *invasion* without her awareness nor detection is an astonishing discovery in itself, and Season Three will pick up on this theme of violation with more such bombshells. Nikita is educated in Section's "history" first by Walter and then by Adrian. The effect of the information is to realign our perceptions of the power base. George

and Oversight have lurked in the background as administrative watchdogs in several episodes, but Adrian, as the architect of Section, as the "only person Madeline has ever been afraid of," and as the woman with the larger perspective on Operations' plans for global control carries a mystique and power that is startling and challenges the assumptions upon which the series has been constructed.

Legitimizing Adrian's assertions is the secondary plot-line in which Operations brings in a "ringer" (Ted Atherton's wonderfully officious and unlikable Leeds) to take the fall on an

L — Albert Street behind
    Toronto's Old City Hall
S — Marin's entourage
    travels

L — Albert Street behind
Toronto's Old City Hall,
different angle
S — Marin arrives

assassination secretly designed (by Operations) to fail, contrary to the wishes of George and Oversight. Watson is great as the threatened Madeline puts Leeds through his paces and Glazer's Operations gleefully withholds his game plan. The puzzle of personal and political motivations that binds Madeline and Operations is becoming reflected in overt misunderstandings and pettiness; the simmering conflict between the pair will continue into the third season despite their mutual political support, and will provide the writers with rich dramatic opportunities.

As Section's political underbelly is exposed, so too is its hidden physical structure, which proves unexpectedly vulnerable to Nikita and Adrian's infiltration (another *violation*). As Nikita pieces together the new information with her experiences, the camera also tries to give us the whole picture with numerous "fish-eye" lens shots of different areas of Section. Nikita's exploration leads her to hidden levels, rooms, and data storage areas. These new and richly detailed sets are introduced here in the finale and contribute to the overall feeling that things will never be the same again in Section.

Music

"Gun" by **Gus Gus** from *Polydistortion* (Warner Brothers) — Michael looks for Nikita

Guest Cast

Siân Phillips (Adrian), Anais Granofsky (Carla), Geoff Murrin (Steven), Ted Atherton (Leeds)

222 END GAME

Written by Robert Cochran & David Ehrman
Directed by Joseph L. Scanlon

Nikita's work for Adrian is revealed to be a Section ploy designed to lure Adrian and her forces into the open. But Nikita has learned more than Operations bargained for and she puts Section "on trial" for its crimes.

Nikita is taking bigger risks all the time. When Walter comes across her it is startling, but when she trips an alarm there is a heart-pounding sequence as Nikita (directed by the cool-headed Adrian) dispatches one colleague and frames another for her crimes. Her poker face remains intact throughout, but Michael's uncanny instincts kick in and his suspicions are raised. The deceit puts him in the impossible position of having to turn her in to Operations. It could be a moment that turns the audience against him but the visible pain he endures because of Nikita's lies, his repeated offers of help or escape (on no less than three occasions), and his final public display of affection more than redeem him. They serve to humanize him even further and deepen the tragic proportions of their relationship.

Peta Wilson and Roy Dupuis do some great work in this episode. The scene in Nikita's apartment is heart-breaking. Wilson is perfect as Nikita's words deny any knowledge of Adrian while her eyes betray the pain of her lies. Dupuis is even better as Michael rides an emotional roller coaster as he shows anger (at Nikita's lies), disbelief and puzzlement (at her motivations), shock and wonder (at the revelations of the double- and triple-cross), interest (in Operations' explanations for Section's alliances), relief (at the resolution of the stand-off), and tenderness and resignation (as Nikita stands her ground and awaits her fate). The actor plays the emotions in a highly controlled manner and the tension is hypnotic. Finally, Michael's statement that Section "sent me but they don't control me" is a

L — Toronto's City Hall, Nathan Phillips Square
    (Queen and Bay Streets)
S — Nikita enters and finds contact on a stretcher

Inset:
L — East side of Nathan Phillips Square
S — Nikita leaves Adrian in the limo and
    approaches along the walkway

L — Unwin Avenue and Leslie Street
S — Nikita plants the KL6

surprising insight into how Michael sees himself and prepares the way for the trials of the next season.

Patterns of threes emerge throughout the hour. Michael's three offers of help, three operatives are originally suspected of treason, there is the triangle of the old guard (Adrian, Operations, and Madeline) and of the newest collusion (Nikita, Operations, and Madeline), and there is, of course, the overriding triple-cross. Nikita penetrates the very core of Section to retrieve the "Gemstone" file, but there is a touch of humor when she takes advantage of her access to check up on where Michael lives. When she first enters the room and scans the databanks she reads a scenario marked the "Invasion of Canada." It is a clever industry wink acknowledging the proliferation of U.S. shows that shoot in Canada (including this one) and it is particularly funny for Canadian viewers (sensitive to the impact American culture has in Canada) who will recall from high school history lessons that Canadian soldiers sent the Americans packing in the War of 1812!

Nikita's final decision to side with her overlords is swayed by personal experience rather than the somewhat specious political argument that Hussein's presence in the Middle East is preferable to the alternatives suggested by Section's "sims" and forecasts. It is a decision that is consistent with her personality and creates the rich dramatic possibilities of the Season Three opener. More importantly though, it does not remove the shadow of doubt cast by Adrian upon Operations' motivations.

Music

Original music by Sean Callery

Guest Cast

Siân Phillips (Adrian), Anais Granofsky (Carla), Jim/Geoff Murrin (Steven), Roger Honeywell (Ames)

SEASON THREE

301 LOOKING FOR MICHAEL

Written by Michael Loceff
Directed by Jon Cassar

Operations and Madeline begin to "clean house" in the wake of Adrian's death. Nikita struggles to stay alive while she looks for Michael, who is absent from Section on a deep-cover assignment.

Season Three's opener closes out the Nikita-Adrian story arc and introduces a four-part arc for Michael's character. Writer Michael Loceff and director Jon Cassar kick the season into high gear with a marvelous action-packed mission designed to rid the Section of Nikita (its bothersome conscience) once and for all. Peta Wilson and her stunt double kick some serious Section ass here and the visuals are great. There is a feminine, almost magical and hypnotizing moment when Nikita's bamboo hat spins with its blue ribbons through the air, hovers, and lands still turning. It is an image that stands in sharp contrast to Nikita's lean and economical black form as she emerges to counter her ambush, both barrels blazing. This new image of feminine power eludes her executioners by sliding down a cargo chute (echoes of her original restaurant escape down a garbage chute in the pilot episode), attacks from the ceiling of a freight elevator, jumps through a glass window, makes a multi-story drop to the roof of a car, does the splits to avoid the bullets being shot upwards from within, does a backwards somersault over the trunk of the car, and lands feet down and shoots out the back window in the same motion! It's no wonder

Facing page:
L — Door to private residence in Mississauga, Ontario
S — Door to Michael's house

Operations and Madeline finally put off her demise.

Birkoff is certainly emerging as a cool customer. His discovery of Madeline and Operations' vulnerability to Oversight, his plan to steal Chris' iris pattern, his planting of evidence to incriminate Chris, and his nail-biting close-call in the elevator as he steals and transmits data to George all speak to an expertise and rather eerie self-control. Birkoff has grown considerably from the agoraphobic, technocentric cynic to a professional, careful, and caring member of Nikita's coterie.

Operations and Madeline begin the year with new looks, new vulnerabilities, and a new flexibility. Their savagery and instincts for self-preservation are still intact as they begin to eliminate all witnesses to Adrian's infiltration of Section and subsequent capture. Watson and Glazer are wonderful as their characters, backs to the wall, discuss their need to divert the suspicions of George (David Hemblen in a quietly threatening turn) and their difficulties in exterminating Nikita with more than a hint of Lord and Lady Macbeth about them.

The real revelation, of course, is Nikita's discovery of Michael's home, complete with wife and child, a "blood cover" that has been in effect for many years and an ingenious dramatic invention by Surnow and the *La Femme Nikita* writing team. What a marvelous way to begin what will be the show's most inventive season yet!

Music

"Temple Caves" by **Mickey Hart** from *Planet Drum* (Rykodisc) — Nikita on a mission

Guest Cast

Samia Shoaib (Elena), Raoul Trujillo (Ferrera), David Hemblen (George), Evan Caravela (Adam), Roland Rothchild (Vince)

302 SOMEONE ELSE'S SHADOW

Written by Michael Loceff
Directed by René Bonnière

Nikita moves in with Michael and his family as Section begins to set into motion a plan to capture Elena's estranged father, terrorist Salla Vacek.

Domesticity is the theme in this episode. It opens with home movies of Michael and his son planting a tree in the backyard. Memories normally meant to be cherished are only cruel ironies accompanied by his emotionless voice-over (as he describes to Nikita the nature of his real mission to capture Vacek). Vacek has no home; leading the life of a nomad he moves from safe-house to safe-house in an attempt to elude the law. Nikita moves in with Michael and Elena (posing as family), joining someone else's household. This, in turn, gives her a front-row seat to the "happy family" and reminds her of a home she can never have (with echoes of Nikita and Michael's brief period of domesticity in "Psychic Pilgrim"), a normalcy which is as elusive to her as it is an illusion for Elena.

The emerging reality over the next two episodes is that Michael truly loves his wife and child. This is not wholly unexpected, considering the barbarity of Section life. (Imagine the tenderness he showed Lisa in "Obsessed" magnified across years with a wife and a child.) Samia Shoaib illuminates Elena as a woman possessed of a wise and loving heart with a quiet strength of spirit. It is not surprising that given such an opportunity Michael would seize whatever happiness he could.

Nikita and Michael's conversation about Simone raises a question about the nature of that marriage also. How is it that this mythologized love of Michael's life coexisted with his life with Elena without his knowing how Simone *felt* about it? And how is it that he fell in love with Nikita while he had such an arrangement at home? These

Left:
L — James Street looking south to Queen Street
S — Nikita's multi-story dive

Bott
L — Etienne Brûlé Park, Old Mill R
S — Michael and Elena await Vacek's arr

are questions without answers, but there is an air of truth about his declaration that he wished he could have told Nikita about it. In the final analysis, the harsh reality is that life in Section is their only reality and it is evident by Nikita's growing restraint that she has accepted this to be true.

Music

"Please This Life" by **Mandalay** from *Please This Life* [single, b-side] (V2 Records, Chrysalis Music) — Nikita thinks about Michael

Guest Cast

Samia Shoaib (Elena), Evan Caravela (Adam), Hrant Aliank (Vacek), John Bourgeois (Misha), Barry MacGregor (Williams), Henry Allessandroni (Beckman)

303 OPENING NIGHT JITTERS

Written by David J. Burke
Directed by Jon Cassar

Elena is poisoned by Section while Michael is on a mission after he refuses to do it himself. The ruse lures Vacek to the hospital where he is executed by a Section operative, who also fakes Michael's murder.

Madeline and Operations hit a new low on the humanity scale (if they even register on that scale any longer) when they order Michael to poison his wife and order Nikita to provide surveillance and act as a witness. This unique horror, we learn, is to catch a uniquely elusive criminal, but the depravity of the act is so extreme that not only does Michael refuse the order (after sabotaging his sole attempt) but he states he will kill his overseers if Elena dies. The threat stands as the

L — Central Hospital (333 Sherbourne Street)
S — Vacek visits Elena in the hospital

first time Michael has overtly expressed his opinion of Madeline and Operations or their actions. Their baseness is matched only by their smug condescension at the hour's conclusion (acknowledging Michael's sacrifice). One shudders to think what the "Level 9" proposal will entail.

The episode also gives us a glimpse into the warmer side of a strangely controlled family environment. The irresistibly cute Adam (played warmly by young Evan Caravela) plays at passing for thirty to win a taste of wine from his father, and writer David J. Burke adds a nice touch when Adam asserts he has learned karate all by himself at school. It's a bittersweet notion that the boy has the character to excel on his own without the aid of a father (a martial arts expert) whose very presence is a cover for a mission.

The production and prop departments show off some new gadgets here too, particularly a remote holographic interrogation device for Madeline. Beautifully shot and intensely creepy, the scene is a veritable gadget-fest. Still it's "nice" to see the torture twins out in the field and inflicting something other than coercive pain. Mick Schtoppel becomes a permanent fixture as Nikita's new neighbor, and unfortunately his presence will be played for an often jarring comic relief. But here his presence in the next-to-last scene gives Nikita an acquaintance with whom she actually shares a point of reference.

When Michael is kidnapped and brought to Vacek while Elena lies dying in the hospital, Roy Dupuis, with writer Burke and director Cassar, creates a powerful multi-colored scene. Michael acts out the mission scenario knowing it is his only chance of saving his wife, but his frustration at being parted from her for so long is evident. He pleads to be let go and his mystified "Who are you?" stops just short of indignant. He could just as easily be demanding such an explanation from Madeline and Operations as they play god with these lives. His pain is as real as is his shame when, having lured Vacek out of hiding, he can barely look at the man he has just defeated. Dupuis shines here, stretching his acting muscles and offering a glimpse of this actor's marvelous range.

Music

"Chanson Sans Issue (Ne Vois-Tu Pas)" by **Autour de Lucie** from *Immobile* (Nettwerk) — Nikita sit in a chair (intro)
"Is Jesus Your Pal" by **Gus Gus** from *Polydistortion* (Warner Brothers) — Michael walks the streets

Guest Cast

Samia Shoaib (Elena), Evan Caravela (Adam), Hrant Aliank (Vacek), John Bourgeois (Misha), Henry Allessandroni (Beckman), Carlo Rota (Mick Schtoppel)

304 GATES OF HELL

Written by Robert Cochran
Directed by René Bonnière

Michael's trademark control unravels as his shock gives way to grief at the loss of his son. Nikita tries to protect Michael from Operations' growing impatience; and Birkoff discovers a hidden file that could prove damaging to Operations and Madeline.

The opening four-part arc concludes with Michael's journey through and out of an emotional hell. Hollowed out by grief, Michael sits alone in an apartment as empty as himself and as stripped of furniture as he is of a reason to live. Director René Bonnière and Roy Dupuis create a painful scene as Michael views his precious home movies of Adam and contemplates suicide. The musical soundtrack for this scene is inspired. Its near *a capella* quality reflects Michael's spare physical space and the childlike vocals act as a counterpoint to Michael's emotional torment, while seeming almost comforting at the same time. It is truly shocking to see Michael *so* out of control, emotional, and exposed in front of everyone.

Dupuis is marvelous throughout the episode. His restraint usually sets the tone and the style for any scene he is in (and, his co-stars have said, for the production itself). Gone now is Michael's usual economy of movement as he arrives late for a briefing, fusses with a chair, and gets smart-assed with Operations. There is even humor in Michael's "Thank-you" to Operations' sarcastic "Nice of you to join us" and his "Why not?" in answer to Nikita's question "Should we attack?" Michael may as well be at a picnic, he's so disinterested in the mission. And there is a wonderful moment when Michael, whose nerves have been rubbed raw, jumps at the gunfire he hears as he observes the episode's first mission. Later, Michael, unable to kill himself, awaits his fate, alarms turned off and unconcerned as he plays the cello for his absent son. (Dupuis learned the piece for the show, which sadly had to be dubbed in by another performer due to technical problems with the recording.) Nikita, guarding Michael by night, plays Beatrice to Michael's Dante, hoping to lead him out of hell and give him a will to survive, perhaps reciprocating in some part Michael's help with her own "dark night of the soul" in "Brainwashed." It is ironic that although Michael's newfound depth of understanding enables him to tell Brevich what he needs to know (that the man who killed his son is dead), it is with barely a flicker that he executes the man.

It speaks to Operations' emotional vacuity that a potential point of identification between the two men (they've both lost sons) becomes merely a point of correction in a cruelly familiar exchange between the men. (Operations employs the same phrasing used by Michael to Nikita in "Spec Ops": "get over it.") Operations' ham-fisted attempts to jolt Michael back from introspection generate criticism and a plea for caution from Madeline. There is a curious and intriguing statement by Madeline that she knows "better" than Operations that there is no "pulling back" in their line of work. This season we will see more conflict of this kind and gain more insight into the duo's power structure. Connected by ruthlessness, they are a balance of his emotion and her control. But this time Madeline's attempts to temper Operations' impatience with caution earn her a lecture on god's fallibility.

Birkoff's discovery of the "umbrella file," a leftover file from the Adrian debacle, reinforces his assertions that the governing pair are vulnerable. But it doesn't really seem credible that Operations would have forgotten a file so soon after Birkoff used (hidden) information to prevent Nikita's execution (in "Looking for Michael"). It is also a shame that, because of awkward scene construction, we don't share Birkoff's discovery that he and Walter have been bluffed by Operations in their botched blackmail attempt.

Michael's domestic/mission situation is a clever answer to the inevitable fan questions about how long the lovers will remain apart.

But the "cheat" to explain Michael's distant emotional stance with respect to Nikita (and that Nikita has really been pursuing a married man without knowing it) will give the writers an even greater challenge with the obstacles now removed that once kept them apart. Writer Robert Cochran's chilling finale, as Operations delivers his little hunting dog homily, provides the blueprint for the course of Nikita and Michael's tribulations for the rest of the season.

Music

"Is Jesus Your Pal" by **Gus Gus** from *Polydistortion* (Warner Brothers) — Michael grieves the loss of his son

Guest Cast

Edward Evanto (Brevich)

305 IMITATION OF DEATH

Written by Cyrus Nowrasteh
Directed by Brad Turner

When Nikita goes undercover to capture a scientist who has been brainwashing children to act as assassins, she discovers he has begun experiments that will allow him to genetically design and then clone his creations. To her horror she also discovers that Section has perfected the procedure and that she has already been cloned herself.

Madeline and Operations play it very close to the chest in the wake of the recent shows of independence by Nikita, Michael, and Birkoff. Operations starts to make good on his promise to keep Birkoff in line ("Looking for Michael") when he sets up Felix as a shadowy threat. Nice handheld camera work and a fisheye lens impart Birkoff's growing sense of claustrophobia and paranoia. And we are treated to a taste of "Section mythology" when Walter explains that there are stories that abeyance operatives sometimes escape their death sentences. Matthew Ferguson and Alberta Watson have some fun together as Madeline plays with Birkoff's head: he talks himself into the idea that the Felix situation is really a "test" as she lets him chase his own tail. And, in a rare pairing, Birkoff approaches Michael for help. Unmoved by Birkoff's plight and his past loyalties, Michael offers cold comfort and terse advice: "Don't let him [kill you]."

More and more, Nikita is emerging as a willing participant in her own fate when, in danger, she insists that the raid on Chernov's lab is aborted to give her time to continue her investigation. Nikita has been the victim of both emotional and psychological exploitation during past missions, but here (and in the next episode) she falls prey to an elemental violation when one of her eggs is harvested by the scientist, Chernov. The "rape" is made all the more disturbing when Nikita discovers Section has beaten Chernov in his race to create his own Brave New World and when we observe Michael listening impassively to the whole procedure. It's a voyeurism that echoes Birkoff's in the opening scene. There is something intensely creepy about Birkoff's quiet and unemotional repetition of "kill him" (to the operative transfixed by the eyes of an eighteen-year-old suicide bomber).

Eugene Lipinski exudes quiet power as the soft-spoken, diabolical villain, Ivan Chernov, leader of his own very Section-like organization. Is it asexuality or singularity of focus that drives his disinterest in an unclothed Nikita? Whatever the reason, it is a disinterest he shares with the Inquisitor of "Cat and Mouse," strangely ironic considering the depth of the violations these two villains perpetrate on Nikita.

After two seasons of manipulations, the audience is pretty savvy to the writers' tricks and sleights of hand, so nobody is fooled when Nikita is apparently betrayed by Michael and sold to the scientist, Chernov. But writer Cyrus Nowrasteh compensates for audience expectations by adopting a more subtle approach in this episode. By

the end of the hour, Nikita, Michael, Birkoff, and the audience have all been deceived by the machinations of Operations and Madeline and we are left to wonder at the complex wheels within wheels of Section life. Why does Nikita believe Madeline when she is told her egg was destroyed in Chernov's lab? What is Section's plan for their own crop of children? Have they become so tired of dealing with unruly self-assertive operatives that they have decided to grow their own? Why would they clone Nikita who has been a thorn in the side of Section since Day One? Another wonderful zero resolution story!

Music

"Sunset Bell" by **Love Spiral Downwards** from *Flux* (Projekt) — wordless chant

Guest Cast

Eugene Lipinski (Chernov), Michael Gabriel (Felix), Shawn Roberts (Milan)

306 LOVE AND COUNTRY

Written by Lawrence Hertzog
Directed by Ted Hanlan

Another little surprise from Operations' past: he has a wife who is still alive and now married to a political leader with possible ties to terrorist funds seeking election. When Nikita infiltrates Markali's campaign headquarters and is ordered to seduce the man, she begins to suspect Operations' actions are motivated by emotion rather than justice.

In keeping with *La Femme Nikita's* tradition of open endings, we get an ambiguously motivated tale to the end. Operations is uncharacteristically forthcoming with the team about his personal connection to the mission right from the beginning. Even Madeline is unsure that

Operations' motives are above board and by the episode's end, it remains unclear what his motivations have been, even though it is determined that Markali's ties to the Baddenheim group are deep and long-lived. With nothing more to go on than his gut instinct, Operations takes on George (with whom he seems to be constantly having a phone argument) and Madeline.

Cherie Lunghi guest stars in the less-than-fulfilling role of Corrine, a woman driven nuts by Section trickery. She has a great time chewing up the furniture (and knocking it down and cowering behind it) as she takes Corrine on her descent into a chemically-induced homicidal madness. It is a rare treat to see Madeline in the field outside Section, aptly posing as a shrink. Unfortunately, the promise of seeing these two fine actresses together is never particularly fulfilled. In the final analysis (no pun intended), however, it's a rather tawdry tale (typified by Madeline's assertion that "every man is interested in cheating on his wife") that leans more towards Harlequin than Hitchcock.

Writer Lawrence Hertzog (creator of the excellent but short-lived series *Nowhere Man*) tightens the tension between Madeline and Operations, and Watson and Glazer have a field day as the bickering couple. Second Unit director Ted Hanlan takes the helm as director for this episode and does create some wonderful moments while generating a claustrophobic and uneasy mood for the episode. One of those great moments occurs when Nikita verbalizes to Birkoff what everyone is wondering about Operations' motives. Operations shoots her a look from across the Great Hall that is virtually demonic.

That Operations was an intelligence officer in the military when he went MIA comes as no great surprise, and it's a nice little bone to throw the audience. But once again we are left with more questions than answers. Is Operations' willingness to sacrifice Corrine done in the name of political rectitude or as a punishment for not remaining the dutiful "little woman"? The episode is an interesting, albeit dubious, essay on domestic fidelity. What is Operations feeling as he observes his incapacitated ex-wife from afar? Does he need to satisfy himself as to the results of manipulations or is he hoping for more than the glimpse of recognition he seems to get? These unanswered questions go a long way towards shoring up the mystery of Operations' power and unworldly strength and mitigating the potential damage of seeing Operations and Madeline as middle management (vulnerable to attacks from everyone from Oversight to Birkoff).

Music

Original music by Sean Callery

Guest Cast

Cherie Lunghi (Corrine), David McIlwraith (Markali), Silvio Oliviero (Caspi), James Binkley (Charles)

307 CAT AND MOUSE

Written by Ed Horowitz
Directed by Terry Ingram

Nikita is captured on a mission and replaced by a lookalike whom she must "coach" to pass as herself in Section.

He's baack!

The Inquisitor returns. It's great to see James Faulkner again but one has to wonder just why he's been brought back. Lacking the menace of his first appearance in "War," he seems rather toothless in his little wheelchair issuing threats against Michael's life. (Although it is interesting to get Inquisitor's "outside" observation that Nikita is "becoming more confident in [her] work.") As fun as it is to watch, the episode is not particularly tense. By now the audience knows too many of the personal "secrets" that can only, and inevitably do, trip up the impostor and her mentor. Let's not forget that the Inquisitor's files are two years out of date; he was fooled by the relationship two years ago and again here when he, humorously, assumes a normalcy between Nikita and Michael that has never been there. The idea of creating a duplicate Nikita (Abby) and replacing the real one is an intriguing idea — so fitting as a Red Cell plan — but the episode airs too soon after the cloning themes of "Imitation of Death."

Still, it really *is* a fun episode to watch. Writer Ed Horowitz, playing with the all-too-familiar "evil twin" convention, gives us, perhaps, more of a "shadow self" for Nikita as Abby acts out behavior in Nikita's place that is not such a huge stretch of the imagination. Her roll in the hay with Birkoff is a wet-dream-come-true for him that is very sweetly resolved in the final act by Nikita. Abby's night of pleasure with Michael is appropriately upsetting for the viewer and creates an awkwardness for Nikita and Michael — the effects of which remain unclear in the final scene.

By remaining within the confines of a credible storyline, the episode gives "Abby," and consequently Wilson herself, little room to explore a distinctly different character. Abby's deception allows for only subtle betrayals of character such as the occasional sly grin to remind us that she is *very* pleased with herself. It is a shame that Wilson is not given the same opportunity to play against type as Dupuis had in playing an amnesiac Michael in "Not Was."

Rocco Matteo's simple yet visually striking set is shot from above affording a full view of Nikita (on a leash!) within her circle of movement and creating a visual metaphor for her life inside Section. In the final showdown, she uses her restricted motion effectively as a weapon to lash out and disarm her captor (yet another metaphor for Nikita's current penchant for working *within* her boundaries). The snappy editing from Richard Wells, as our point of view shifts between Nikita and Abby, is admirably seamless.

And we are treated to another classic La Femme Nikita open ending. Does Nikita follow Madeline's advice and execute Abby and, therefore, her alter ego/shadow-self/self (a sight we've already had in another form when Abby shoots Nikita with the dart)? And what will be the lasting effects of such an experience? Abby's presence was not merely a displacement and a violation, but also a possession of sorts which Madeline proposes can only be exorcised through violence (this of course says more about Madeline than the possession). And what of Nikita's torturer? One thing is certain: The sight of Abby/Nikita's cancellation is more than Michael has the stomach for as he averts his gaze in the final shot.

Music

"Lamb" by **Gorecki** on *Lamb* (Mercury Records) — Michael and "Nikita" in bed

Guest Cast

James Faulkner (Inquisitor)

308 OUTSIDE THE BOX

Written by Jim Korris
Directed by Gord Langevin

When Nikita participates in the frame-up of an innocent man (recruited by Section because of his photographic memory) she begins to question the chain of events that led to her own presence inside Section.

Benjamin Kruger is a fascinating character in the hi-tech world of *La Femme Nikita*. He is the ultimate *anti-gadget, anti-tech* invention with his perfectly developed photographic memory. As such, he comments aptly on the very heart of Section One. By creating their tech-resistant

L — Cherry Restaurant (Cherry and Commissioners)
S — Karl and Nikita's hideout

security system, Section's enemies have forced Operations to rely on the human factor. Highly ironic for an organization built on the systematic devaluation of singularity and the subjugation of the human; and how humorous that the very act of valuing humanity and individuality over technology and uniformity is acknowledged as "thinking outside the box" for Section.

Their shared individualism, innocence and, as we learn, "shadow recruitment" draw Nikita and Kruger together. It is no wonder that they hit it off so quickly. The wonderful on-screen chemistry between Peta Wilson and guest star Christopher Bolton is evident throughout, most especially in Nikita's make-nice scene with Kruger (his characterization of her as "some kinda martial arts chick" earns him an enjoyable slap on the backside) and during the mission sequence — shot in blood reds — as both operatives do their jobs "very well."

Nikita's appeal to their common humanity sways the Section One operative in Belgrade who holds the key to her presence in Section, but — no surprise here — holds none in her dealings with Madeline and Michael. Michael has some distance to go before he can shake his reputation as Operations' and Madeline's messenger boy.

The seeds of "Any Means Necessary" and "Three-Eyed Turtle" are planted here as Greg Hillinger (Kris Lemche) returns to taunt Birkoff and live up to the promise of his genius in "Fuzzy Logic." By creating a no-win situation for Birkoff by framing Tatyana, Hillinger defines the challenge that lays ahead for Birkoff.

More and more, this season the *La Femme Nikita* writers will demand that we think outside the box. In black-and-white sequences (which include both footage repeated from the first episode, "Nikita," and unaired and newly shot footage), Nikita remembers the orchestrated events that turned her world upside down. The intriguing question of just why Nikita is in Section is left hanging, as is the answer to the question of why there have been so many attempts to eliminate her. Writer Jim Korris does for the original premise of the series what Lenkov will do for the love story ("under the influence"); he turns it on its head and demands that Nikita, and we, re-think the events surrounding her imprisonment and recruitment by Section.

Music

"Superstar" by **Vibrolux** on *Vibrolux* (Shoreline Records) — Nikita in the bar with Dobbs and Kruger

"Ride with the Flow" by **Sixty Channels** on *Tuned In . . . Turned On* (World Domination) — Nikita in the bar

"Revenge" by **Thrive** on *Thrive* (Spider) — Nikita recalls her life on the streets and the murder in the alley

Guest Cast

Kris Lemche (Greg Hillinger), Christopher Bolton (Kruger), Lara Rhodes (Tatyana), James Downing (Scar Man)

309 SLIPPING INTO DARKNESS

Written by Peter M. Lenkov
Directed by Rick Jacobson

After slipping Operations a psychotropic drug, Michael takes control of Section.

Cinematographer David Perrault and director Rick Jacobson create an opening scene of surreal beauty that belies the ugly disintegration to come as a drugged and deranged Operations runs amok in Section. Peter Lenkov's well-constructed tale is a futuristic *Caine Mutiny* of sorts. With the characters performing for hidden Red Cell cameras, the writer employs a clever dramatic device that draws the audience into the story as a virtual participant. We are used to watching Nikita try to unravel the tangle of deceptions, but now we too are the puzzle solvers. There are no "tells" or winks to the audience this time and the camera no longer gives us hints about who knows what.

Section "performs" well for the cameras, offering some interesting psychological insights into the organization's power structure. Michael has a wonderful public "father-son" coming-of-age moment with Operations when he allows Operations to hit him twice, but no more. Madeline's face is a study as Michael orders her removal along with Operations'. Wilson and Dupuis create one of those blood-draining moments when Michael recaptures Nikita for "interrogation and cancellation" — it seems like another in an escalating series of betrayals. The real joy here lies in watching the chaos of Operations' disintegration, the "safely" acted-out fantasy of his removal from power, and the puzzle of who really knows what and when.

The premise of Michael's betrayal is not easily swallowed by an audience attuned to watching the weekly Section "chess matches" — although there is a certain symmetry to the act when one recalls how Operations ordered Michael to poison his wife's drink earlier this season. Eugene Robert Glazer does a marvelous job taking Operations through his paranoid delusions to the brink of madness. In particular, he shoots Nikita a look so crazed and hateful that it knocks her backwards from across the room. It is a grotesque cartoon of Adrian's picture of him as a power-hungry megalomaniac. Adding to the tension is the fact that Operations is a truly powerful individual whose orders are followed without question; given Operations' already evident dislike of Nikita, Madeline and Michael have taken a huge risk setting up Nikita as the voice of protest. Although rational dissuasion by Madeline has saved Nikita's life before, Michael remains wary throughout and accelerates the process when she is in imminent danger. Even Birkoff earns himself a swat (betraying, perhaps, Operations' growing animosity towards him).

Schtoppel's scene seems over the top and an odd note in this otherwise dark and suspenseful story. It is virtually purposeless (as is the final expository scene between Nikita and Michael) except that we hear once again that Nikita and Michael's relationship is a topic of gossip *outside* Section. Even Philo's henchman refers to it. And as Nikita's "execution" is written into the plan, we can deduce that Section is also aware that this is a known quantity (leftover intel from "War"?). Regardless, it is no surprise that such a daring and convoluted plan is employed to snag a Red Cell agent. What a great nemesis the group has proven itself to be.

Music

Original music by Sean Callery

Guest Cast

Carlo Rota (Schtoppel), Brian Tree (Philo), Michael Dyson (Black)

Right:
L — Alley near Spadina and College
(behind the Silver Dollar)
S — Nikita returns to the alley where she
hung out as a street kid

Below:
L — The Silver Dollar Room,
    Spadina Avenue, north of College
S — Nikita picks up Kruger

310 UNDER THE INFLUENCE

Written by Peter M. Lenkov
Directed by Rick Jacobson

Nikita goes undercover again, this time as the supposed fiancée of a terrorist named Karl Peruze, whom Section has given temporary amnesia. The goal is to flush out the location of Karl's brother Simon, who has stolen a stash of anthrax missiles.

Just when you thought you were beginning to understand the depths of Madeline and Operations' plots, along comes the "Casper Project," the hilariously named plan to tie Nikita and Michael together and indoctrinate Nikita with thoughts of duty, love, obedience, and trust through the use of subliminal images. One has to wonder whether Michael has the same influences working on his psyche. The scheme, we learn, has been in effect for over a year, so the timeline begs one question: Why bother to keep them together when so much overt energy has been spent in keeping them apart? Or is this all part of Operations' larger plan to control the pair through his threatened system of rewards and punishments? It is likely that the exercise of control is its own goal — it is certainly succinctly telegraphed in the first shot of Nikita wearing her leash-like choker!

Peta Wilson does some wonderful work here. She is heartbreaking in her crisis scene when she awakens in bed next to Karl, distraught at the notion she has just slept with him. The true level of her horror is not fully evident until her scene with Walter, as she tells him of her out-of-control emotions and he explains their source. For the third time in four episodes, she has become the victim of a shocking violation. It is clear that for her this violation has been the deepest yet, attacking the very core of her being, the one place she felt she was free of Section's influence and choices. Wilson also shines in the shocking and truthful scene in which she slaps Michael for his part in the manipulation. The moment epitomizes the central

Top:
L — Scarborough Bluffs (from Bluffer's Park)
S — Siberian mission

Above:
L — Osgoode Hall (Queen Street and University Avenue)
S — Michael collects the toxin

conflict of her free will and his obedience.

Peter Lenkov's imaginative story boldly calls into question one of the series' primary conceits: the Nikita-Michael love story. Consequently, it is easy to forgive him several serious plot holes. (How does Karl get to Simon's location? He certainly couldn't have asked him where they both have been living. And how is it that Birkoff and Madeline are aware of Steven Wolfe's identity when Operations went to such pains to keep it a secret in "Missing"?) Once again, we are treated to some classic larger-than-life villains in Karl and Simon Peruze (played by wrestler Val Venis). They are monstrous in their delight in torture, murder, and rape. Alan Van Sprang is wonderful as Karl, believable both as the ruthless terrorist and the pliant amnesiac. The often touchy issue of memory loss accompanied by a personality change is handled well here. Van Sprang's scenes with Alberta Watson are fabulous; particularly humorous is Karl's attack on Madeline's vanity as she is rejected by her observant prisoner in the White Room.

In the powerful subplot, Operations learns that his son Steven Wolfe has been murdered by the "green-listed" Martelli. Eugene Robert Glazer is wonderful as he wanders ashen-faced through Section awaiting his opportunity to avenge his son's death. Hard upon the heels of the loss of his ex-wife to madness (however orchestrated by Operations himself) comes the death of his son. With no remaining family to "humanize" Operations or his motivations, his already intense and problematic relationship with Madeline runs the risk of becoming our sole window into his character. Madeline's political savvy is evident yet again as she allows Operations to have his cake and eat it too, while winning favor with George (and even keeping the budget-cutting administrative types at bay). Her protection of Operations is not dissimilar to Nikita's protection of Michael in "Gates of Hell." The issue of Steven's death raises one of the series' central paradoxes: how does one reconcile private sacrifice with the public good, personal revenge with political ambition?

Music

"Eden" by **Hooverphonic** on *Blue Wonder Power Milk* (Sony Music) — Nikita, upset, looks in the mirror

Guest Cast

Val Venis (Simon Peruze), Alan Van Sprang (Karl Peruze), David Hemblen (George)

311 WALK ON BY

Written by Michael Loceff
Directed by René Bonnière

As Walter pursues a girlfriend from his "old life," Nikita's past walks in right through Section's great hall in the person of Jamie, someone from the old neighborhood, who tells Nikita that her mother has stopped drinking and has hired detectives to search for her.

Michael Loceff and René Bonnière team up again to deliver a truly heartbreaking story of past lives, identity, and forgiveness. While Madeline and Operations scheme to control Walter's attempt to contact an old girlfriend, they seemingly miss Michael's efforts to help Nikita reconcile with her mother. Michael's new openness (introduced through his invitation to Nikita to share some down time) encourages her to ask for his help. It's a gift of trust and vulnerability that even *he* cannot turn away from. While the scene is moving, it is also extremely disturbing. Nikita seems willing to abide by the Section rules that would see her mother killed. This submission lends the drama its tragic proportions and perhaps, influences Michael's decision to help.

Walter's need to connect with his past gives us some insight into the long-term effects of working for a place "that doesn't exist." At some point, without that outside reference, he has come to feel that perhaps he also does not exist. His meeting with "Lita" reminds him

of a time when he forged an identity in the outside world — how typical of Walter that his touchstone is one of the heart: an old girlfriend. Of course, identity issues are muddied Section-style for both Walter and Nikita: Beverly poses as Lita, Lita's pictures are altered by Madeline. Nikita disguises herself as a man (with the detective) and as a coma patient (with her mother); and while we learn Nikita's name is Wirth, her worth to Section is still shrouded in mystery ("Outside the Box"). Fiction and real life intersect in the wonderful pictures of a very young Peta Wilson that serve as the few remnants Roberta has left of her daughter.

Margot Kidder is a real treat as Nikita's mother, Roberta Wirth; as is her real life niece, Janet Kidder (Vizcano of "First Mission"), who plays the young Roberta. Margot Kidder's performance is deeply moving, and in only a few scenes she paints a picture of a woman battered by life and so in need of redemption that she searches for a daughter she has been told is long dead and buried. In order to save her mother's life, Nikita must purposefully continue the lie (of her own death) that was forced upon her by Section. And in affording her mother a last chance at forgiveness, she gives up the only thing for which she has ever longed: her mother's love. Nikita's last tie with her old life is finally severed. The tragedy of the losses these two women endure is crushing as Roberta releases her daughter from life and Nikita releases her mother to life. The superlative story by Loceff and affecting direction from Bonnière make "Walk On By" one of the very best hours of La Femme Nikita.

Music

Original music by Sean Callery

Guest Cast

Margot Kidder (Roberta Wirth), Gabriel Hogan (Jamie), Janet Kidder (Young Roberta), Richard Zeppieri (Parness), Monique Mojica (Beverly)

312 THRESHOLD OF PAIN

Written by Michael Sloan
Directed by Terry Ingram

When a mission goes awry, Nikita and two operatives, Angela and Mark, are captured and tortured until Mark (in a vain attempt to save Angela's life) gives up the location of a Section substation. Although she tries to remedy the situation and prevent Mark's cancellation, Nikita soon finds herself fighting for her own life when Mark accuses her of betraying Section.

Michael Sloan's first script for La Femme Nikita pairs off most of the cast and guest actors to offer an examination of the variety of personal relationships inside (and outside) Section, and to build the argument behind Madeline and Operations' determination to keep Nikita and Michael apart. The episode is something of a morality tale warning of the dangers of love. For Nikita and Michael, Angela and Mark, and even Simon and Caroline, no good can come of it.

Larger-than-life villains Simon and Caroline Craychek encompass many of the combinations in one couple: partners in crime and in sadism, lovers and siblings. Played by Adam Ant — 80s pop-rocker turned actor — Simon embodies Section's apparent profile of perfection: a sadist who is literally devoid of feeling. What a surprise when he doesn't measure up for a place in the organization! Caroline, played by the elegant Guylaine St. Onge, is unfortunately dispatched early without enough screen time.

The union of Mark and Angela raises the issue of just what *is* the big deal for the powers that be with Michael and Nikita's pairing? Of course the question is no sooner asked than answered as Mark breaks position to rescue Angela and Michael breaks protocol and bullies Birkoff into locating Nikita so that *he* might rescue *her* in knightly fashion. The obvious identification between these couples is further emphasized by the implication that Michael empathizes with Mark and

Carlo Rota at the 1999 Close Quarters Standby convention.

Angela's situation and that he feels for Mark's loss and pain. Although Michael stretches his emotional muscles he drastically misreads Nikita's guilt/innocence. Worse yet, in Nikita's eyes his actions (an unconditional offer of help) indicate that he places more value on her survival than her word. The emotional tussle leads to an oddly strained moment between the two. In the end, for Nikita, it seems a trick saves her life, not trust, friendship, or loyalty.

Other pairings include Birkoff and Walter, in a cooler-than-cool scene, who don't let a little thing like a near detonation spoil their appetites for lunch. But all is not what it seems even for this pair: Walter has a crisis of faith and Birkoff, despite the cool facade, further confirms his emerging role as chief rule quoter and by-the-book guy. Not once but *twice* (for Nikita's rescue and Craychek's capture) he cites Section regulations — and it is more likely that fear rather than loyalty motivates his deference to Michael's unsanctioned rule bending. And then there is the original odd couple: Operations and Walter in one of the series' most hilarious moments as Operations fumbles about trying to comfort and praise an insecure Walter. Madeline's cleverly orchestrated moment gives the two actors plenty of fuel for comedy and brilliantly sets up the parallel scene in "Beyond the Pale."

Madeline, "inclined to believe Nikita" despite the superhuman lies of Mark, once again proves herself an astute — and therefore potentially deadly — judge of character. And despite Nikita's serious miscalculation (putting her own value system ahead of a knowledge of Mark's character), she forgives Mark, turns the other cheek, and further establishes herself as the compassionate, forgiving martyr.

Music

"Can't Forget You" by **Moa** from *Universal* (Tommy Boy) — Nikita and Mark are in the club

Guest Cast

Adam Ant (Simon), Guylaine St. Onge (Caroline), Trent McMullen (Mark), Karen Glave (Angela)

313 BEYOND THE PALE

Written by Lawrence Hertzog
Directed by René Bonnière

When Michael is passed over for a promotion to head strategist, Michael and Nikita escape Section in an attempt to ferret out a traitor in the organization.

Nikita and Michael get another test-run at domesticity and fans get the relationship fantasy played out for them in this suspenseful and clever episode from writer Lawrence Hertzog. Long-time viewers will not be surprised that the elaborate plot manipulations are designed to trap Zalman, a Red Cell mole. There are plenty of winks to the audience: Zalman's promotion *over* Michael, Michael's losing his cool with Walter, Michael's abrupt signoff to Zalman indicating that the mission target had advance notice of Section's arrival, Madeline's insight into Michael's behavior, Michael's "capture" on a routine supply run — well, you get the picture.

The contrivance of the hidden cameras is too similar to that of "Slipping into Darkness" (and the upcoming "Three-Eyed Turtle") but it raises the intriguing question of just when did Nikita know what was going on? One could argue Michael informed her when he collected her at her apartment but her rejoinder to Zalman ("If you think about it long enough, it'll come to you") sounds like code for

how she figured it out. She and Michael share a very uncomfortable moment immediately afterwards.

Jamie Harris, brother to Wilson's real-life boyfriend director Damian Harris, guest stars as Zalman, the loathsome, bullying, backstabbing, suck-up, corporate, toady sycophant. He's the man you love to hate, and Harris plays him unsympathetically and with relish. How gratifying that we see him fold like a tent when the tables are finally turned. Harris and Francks have great fun when Walter and Zalman go head to head — first when Zalman begins to throw his weight around and later, in the truly shocking torture scene where Zalman's sadism is fully evident. Harris' performance is particularly enjoyable as he switches postures from petty bully with Walter to dutiful son with Operations.

The real kicker, of course, is Michael's interrogation. Zalman taunts Michael with the promotion, the "blonde whore" comment, and finally with a live satellite feed of his son. This must be an object lesson for Michael, for it conjures up the actual power Operations could wield over Michael if he chose to. In fact, the whole mission is an interesting exercise as it provokes a statement from Michael that sums up the theme of Nikita's journey this season: "In Section you move up or you move out."

Section's corporate mores are the subject of discussion again as Walter and Madeline, members of the "old guard," consider the loss of past values. The conversation builds on Madeline and Operations' exchange in the previous episode, in which the two overtly acknowledge authorship of Section's "usual approach." These exchanges make one wonder what Section was like before the era of Operations. The very idea of a Red Cell mole attaining class-five operative status certainly speaks to Section's vulnerability. So is the approach of the current regime a response to a changing world or is it part and parcel of the change it purportedly fights?

Hertzog's script is filled with wonderful moments. Walter and Operations' honest and open dialogue is a beautiful twin to the

comedic fumble of "Threshold of Pain" and a rare glimpse into why
these men continue to work together. In spite of the dramatic sleight
of hand, Wilson and Dupuis's scenes in the farmhouse (which will
resonate for Dupuis fans who remember the actor makes his home in
the Quebec countryside) and later in Nikita's apartment are moving
and truthful. Nikita and Michael finally achieve moments of honesty
and emotion; tenderness born of a considered desire, not of over-
blown dramatics.

Music

"Ma Jeunesse Fout le Camp" by **Francoise Hardy** on *Ma
Jeunesse Fout le Camp* (EMI) — Nikita plays one of Michael's old
records

Guest Cast

Jamie Harris (Zalman), Michael Cram (Fredericks)

314 HAND TO HAND

Written by Ed Horowitz
Directed by T.J. Scott

*When Nikita goes undercover in a brothel — to help Michael reach and assassinate
Charles Meyer — she discovers that the women there are engaged in a deadly battle for
their lives.*

Fighting fish, fighting chicks, fighting chick executives. What more
could a fan want?

Nikita has been honing her intuition as her premonitory dream
would suggest. Too bad her intuition doesn't tell her to listen to
Madeline more carefully: it is often what Madeline does not say that is
most revealing. The opening shot of Nikita floating in a pool with arms

outstretched, beams radiating from her head, and liturgical choral music underscoring the scene overtly draws on Christian imagery. This episode comments on the ruthless nature of Nikita's work, her life, her survival skills, and her efforts to rescue the innocent. This time she is speaking for those without a voice. The women here are "invisible" and disposable and somehow don't count as victims. They are *so* invisible that Section doesn't even *bother* to collect data on the fights (their duration, location, and survival rate are all incidental to a bored Birkoff). The antagonist, Aurora, played by the exotic Marjean Holden, even remains nameless until the very last scene.

Ed Horowitz's ironic and self-conscious commentary is stylishly directed by T.J. Scott. Matteo's sumptuous sets, photographed by Jim Westinbrink, are filled with jeweled glass, rich fabrics, water, and fish. With the fish bowls catching the light, Aurora and Nikita, dressed in the same red and blue, circle each other under the watchful eye of Michael like the battling fish. As beautiful as the imagery of the fish is, it is overused. Still, the inter-cutting of images during the water battle does contribute beautifully to the claustrophobic chaos of this scene.

The similarity between Section and the brothel — in which the women fight to survive just in order to fight again — is also clear enough without Nikita drawing the parallel. But comparisons are inevitable: Section One's cold, techie environment belies its archaic values and inhumane treatment of operatives and prisoners alike. Here in the brothel, the medieval environment with its pit and shock-control chokers directly reflects these same attitudes towards an expendable and disposable labor supply. While Aurora and Nikita slug it out for real and ostensibly to the death, Madeline and Renée (played by Eugene Glazer's wife Brioni Farrell) fight their battle "in the boardroom." Madeline's use of protocol violations to rid herself of Renée may be less visceral and even pretty bloodless, but the stakes are high enough. Whether it be jealousy or territorial imperative (Renée even intrudes upon the sacred breakfast ritual) the real tug of

war is between Operations and Madeline and over who will control the relationship — a question that seems moot by the end of the episode as Operations blackmails Madeline into a sexually compromising situation.

Nikita and Michael's exchange is restrained and played very low-key. Michael's report to Nikita seems almost rote, with Michael possibly at his most still and motionless. His deference to Nikita's insistence that she stay and help the captive women and the quiet shorthand these two are developing contrasts significantly with Madeline and Operations' more volatile relationship. For Nikita and Aurora, the issue is complicity vs. survival: Aurora does what she has to in order to survive and Nikita (her other self) shows her the way of mercy. And, just in case we missed it the first time, the last shot bookends the opening sequence as Nikita lies back on her couch with a halo of blond hair spread out about her head as she discusses the *miracle* of surviving another day in Section (read *hell*).

Music

Mark Snow's new mix of the opening theme

"Death by Moonlight" by **Rhea Obsession** on *Initiation* (Spider Records) — Nikita's battle in the pool

Guest Cast

Marjean Holden (Aurora), Brioni Farrell (Renée), Kristin Booth (Sandra), David Ferry (Anagar)

315 BEFORE I SLEEP

Written by Peter M. Lenkov
Directed by Joel Surnow

Madeline convinces a dying woman to spend the last weeks of her life helping Section by posing as a terrorist.

Joel Surnow, who reduced his role to creative consultant this season, switches caps this round and takes on the role of director for Peter Lenkov's inventive story. The episode contains a good balance of action sequences, such as the lively opening car scene, and quiet, more intimate scenes like Madeline's recruitment of Sarah and the scene between Michael and Sarah, which features playful and forthright work from Dupuis. Guest star Juliet Landau, as Sarah, insightfully pegs Michael as an unpleasant man used to getting what he wants; Michael is uncharacteristically charmed by this insight rather than threatened. There is even the stylish injection of videotaped footage as Sarah looks through the surveillance glasses for the first time — adding a touch of hyper-realism, as Sarah herself begins to realize the danger she's taken on. Landau (who plays Drusilla on *Buffy the Vampire Slayer*) breathes life into her two creations, Jan and Sarah. One could even argue she has the fun of drawing three characters as the reticent Sarah begins to emerge from her shell.

Ironies abound here, for although Section's use of Sarah as a "wet duplicate" in the final days of her life is an aberration to Nikita, the experience affords the woman her first and only opportunity to act out without real risk. And Madeline's astutely directed appeals to Sarah's sense of duty hold much less weight than Sarah's more personal motivation to go out with a bang (almost literally).

Lenkov's script is littered with lighter moments as well: the female half of the torture twins actually gets some lines, including a clinical discussion of the side effects of one of the latest weapons of persuasion and Nikita's child-like secret smile as Michael admits caring for someone. And it can't really come as a surprise that the attrition rate is high in "housekeeping." Sarah's quick exchange with Walter as she asks for directions to Com is delightful and for the Canadian fans there is a bit of insider trivia: the bomb's security code (416) is the Toronto area code!

In the end though, the cruelest cut is reserved for Nikita herself. Motivated by a misdirected belief in another one of Section's "tricks" she convinces herself (with a bit of help from the quick-thinking Madeline) that Sarah's leukemia was induced artificially — not a big leap considering the cloning science of "Imitation of Death." There is no end to the variety of Section manipulations and this one even has a name (an "incentive scenario"). Wouldn't Nikita love to have a look at the Operations Manual one day, if only to get the rules straight?

Music

"I Feel Free" by **Cream** on *Fresh Cream* (Reaction) — Michael and Nikita follow Jan

Guest Cast

Juliet Landau (Jan/Sarah), Peter Cockett (Ashe), Ron Kennell (Corey), Madhuri Bhatia (Darius)

Above:
L — Front Street, looking east to Church Street and the
    "Flatiron" building
S — Michael and Nikita follow Jan

Above:
L — Scott Street looking south
S — Nikita and Michael follow Jan

Above:
L — Colborne Street and Leader Street looking
    west
S — Jan spies the car and starts her suicide run

Left:
L — Colborne Street looking east
S — Jan takes her suicide run at Nikita and
    Michael

L — Walmer Road
S — Jan meets Marco Ashe

L — #218 Walmer Road
S — Marco Ashe's house

316 I REMEMBER PARIS

Written by Michael Loceff
Directed by Terry Ingram

Operations gives the order to incinerate Section when an agent for Glass Curtain infiltrates Section and transmits Section's Paris location and the encrypted Section directory.

Just when we finally learn where Section is — it isn't!

For some unknown reason writer Michael Loceff brings back Errol Sparks and his sidekick Siobhan (of first season's "Simone"). Awkward exposition by Walter and Nikita in the final act is just not enough to explain the return of Glass Curtain's dynamic duo. A host of unanswered questions arises. Why doesn't Michael react when he learns of Sparks' resurrection, and why is Simone's possible survival never addressed? Sparks' charm is traded in for a few cheesy one-liners and an inside reference to the series' staff writers' addiction to peppermint patties.

Speaking of comic relief, Mick Schtoppel is back, proving himself useful this time (however annoying his exaggerated face-making is as Michael tortures Freddie Allan) not only to Section, but to Nikita herself (sparing her Operations' wrath). One wonders when the other shoe will drop with this character. At least his presence affords Nikita a new foil and provokes Wilson to throw in an ad-libbed "Aussie-ism" as Nikita hurries Mick along with "Snap!"

Nikita is either underfoot or at loose ends throughout the episode, raising the question: just what is Nikita's place in Section? Operations certainly has an opinion on that one: thinking and plotting strategy don't mix with killing and field work. He tells Nikita "you are not here to think," but thinking seems to be her *sole* responsibility when she and Operations enter the field in a rare and dynamic pairing. Just how is Operations planning to impart his feelings about the work done at Section?

L — Behind Osgoode Hall (Queen and University Streets)
S — Michael and Operations leave Section and walk the streets
of "Paris"
(the image of the Eiffel Tower was inserted into this shot.)

Left:
L — Edward Day Gallery,
33 Hazelton Avenue
S — Matteo's Gallery

Below:
L — Edward Day Gallery
S — Operations argues with Nikita

L — Control tower of Downsview Airbase at Sheppard Avenue near Allen Road
S — Freddie Allan's plane arrives

Inset: Long shot of the
Downsview Airbase

Despite the shocking effect of the opener, as Boris gets the jump on the super-human Madeline (employing the same neck hold Madeline applied to Jan in the previous episode), Loceff's script stretches credulity a little too far. The plant of the signal tracker on Boris is much the same ploy Nikita and Adrian used on Michael in order to gain deeper access to Section security — another one of those holes they really *should* do something about. And Boris seems to gain access to *all* of Section's files with relative ease. It took Adrian, Section's architect, several tries to find one file, but this guy grabs them all in minutes.

Still, the premise of the incineration of Section is a bold one and it affords the cast an opportunity to exhibit their trademark cooler-than-cool attitude. When Birkoff laments the move from Paris Walter tells him he can always "visit." Operations and Michael barely acknowledge the upheaval as they depart their home of 24 and nine years, respectively. The sentiment is left for the viewer. After the beautifully edited and frenetic evacuation sequence, director Terry Ingram gives the audience a classic sci-fi moment as the camera lingers over Section's final seconds. The camera work and Sean Callery's grand, monumental, and sentimental score pay homage to *La Femme Nikita*'s seventh character: production designer Rocco Matteo's Section One. Anyone anticipating a new Matteo creation after Operations gave the order to incinerate were quickly disabused of the notion. It turns out that Section compounds, like their inhabitants, are designed to be interchangeable.

Music

"Recitative" by **Christoph William Gluck** (Warner Bros) — classical piece played at Glass Curtain's base

Guest Cast

Julian Richings (Sparks), Ingrid Veninger (Siobhan), Carlo Rota (Schtoppel), Vincent Cocazza (Boris), Deborah Bell (Ellen), Frank Pelleorino (Matteo)

317 ALL GOOD THINGS

Written by Ed Horowitz
Directed by Terry Ingram

Michael and Nikita's newfound closeness falters under the pressures of Michael's formal and temporary promotion to the position of Operations.

Third season's closing arc picks up from the previous episode's dinner scene with the "morning after" (beautifully shot in the warm golden tones of daybreak) and runs to season's end, tracking the trials of the on-again relationship between Nikita and Michael. The

L — View of the docks from Polson Street
S — Nikita chases, shoots, and loses one of Lamaye's men

tenderness and sleepy vulnerability of the sequence stands in sharp contrast to the S&M feel of the lovers' first encounter on the barge in the second season. The timing couldn't be worse, though. Just as Nikita and Michael seem to have reached a common ground and are finally moving in the same direction together (as equals), in steps workplace politics. The public displays of affection are eclipsed by the very public and formal change of command as Operations hands over control of Section to Michael while he is away at "Center" (yet *another* layer of administration and command?).

Michael's attempts to separate his public and private life is an extension of Operations' approach to human resources but it seems to be the only way in which Michael has conformed. He starts thinking rather ably (his layered-matrix solution) and independently (he takes on the Bergomi mission) despite Operations' parting instructions designed to maintain a long-distance control over Michael. The approach leads to conflict with Nikita ("do you want blind obedience or my honest opinion?") who sees her life as an organic whole, not a compartmentalized series of procedures. Their clash mid-mission, in which Nikita refuses his orders and retrieves the hard drive herself, illuminates Michael and Nikita's real strength and the perceived threat felt by Operations and Madeline. Michael's actions also lead inevitably to a stalemate with Operations (much like that of "Last Night"), who sees the Bergomi mission success as a political act of alliance with George. The significance of this perception will be evident by "Three-Eyed Turtle."

Watson and Dupuis do great work together when Michael, unbending in his pursuit of Bergomi, orders Madeline back to work and her face clouds over. Michael is quick to establish and exercise dominance and control over Madeline — invoking the threat his knowledge of Adrian's death implies. When Madeline scuttles off to anemically push Nikita toward a choice between two options (convince Michael to give up the mission or sabotage it) Nikita's strength, as always, is that she believes there is a third choice — thinking outside the box Madeline and Operations want to impose. The episode is also laced with humor: Nikita, suffering from a terminal case of monitor-head after her ten-hour stint in DRV with the over-caffeinated Mintz, is advised by Walter to yell at Michael and "get it out of her system." And there is a new set — the Oversight board room in which the Section heads meet with an increasingly creepy George. His quip about controlling the world conjures an impression that he may just be more dangerous than Operations.

Writer Ed Horowitz gives us an intriguing story that raises a lot of questions about Michael and about the importance of power for Michael, Nikita, Madeline, Operations, and even George. "All Good Things" sets up the issues that will be explored with equal enthusiasm by Michael Loceff in "Third Party Ripoff." Nikita's journey through these two episodes is more subtly explored than Michael's. Michael's loyalty is evident when he names her as his successor even before learning about the dangers of the Odessa mission, but Nikita values her prowess in the field and the loyalty of her fellow mission operatives. Tangled up with her abhorrence of Section's authoritarianism is a respect for Michael's abilities and an attraction to his power. Her place and future in Section remains unclear and a difficult issue for the humanist. One wonders if the bread crumb trail left by the writing team will lead anywhere next season.

Music

"This Love" by **Craig Armstrong (with Elizabeth Fraser)** on *Space Between Us* (Melankolic) — Nikita and Michael "the morning after"

Guest Cast

David Hemblen (George), Sean Sullivan (Mintz)

318 THIRD PARTY RIPOFF

Written by Michael Loceff
Directed by T.J. Scott

Madeline, determined to keep Michael and Nikita apart, begins to strip Michael of his rank and his status inside Section.

In this second of two tales of power, ambition, and identity, writer Michael Loceff offers us a brilliant character study of the enigmatic Michael. (Other members of the cast come under the magnifying glass — quite literally as T.J. Scott frames several shots through the ubiquitous monitor lenses.) Even more fascinating than Loceff's second season "Not Was" — in which Michael, stripped of his memory, exhibited humanity, insecurities, and a personal value system eerily similar to Nikita's — this episode pares away Michael's worldly trappings and reveals a man struggling with how the world sees him, how he sees himself, and how he is perceived by Nikita.

L — Union Station, Front Street (all photos)

Scenes, clockwise from above:
S — The mission begins; Michael stands in front of the
      statue; Michael drops his coat and joins Nikita;
      Michael and Nikita begin "the ripoff" sequence.

With the lessons of "All Good Things" behind him (Nikita's distaste for him in a power position) he seems willing to give it all up in order to hold on to his lover. It is believable that his true goal is to do whatever he does well, including loving Nikita. But it is also clear that, status aside, Michael's creativity in the field is second nature and he can no sooner deny it than stop breathing.

It is chilling to learn the statistics on Madeline's concerns about a dropping "efficiency rate." It must have come as something of a blow to the ego for Nikita to learn that Michael's rate has dropped less than $1\frac{1}{2}$ percent! It does, however, speak to Michael's indisputable discipline and control. Nikita should realize by now that the alliance is seen more as a political threat than an operational one. Madeline plays it out like a game, even naming her strategy the "hard wedge." The fact that it's even named implies that such an eventuality has been anticipated and planned for. One might well wonder if the "hard wedge" is also Madeline's reaction to or revenge for being administratively castrated by Michael in "All Good Things." Once again, it seems doubtful that she can see the world except through the lens of her own reality of power politics.

In a parallel subplot Birkoff and Walter experience a softer "wedge" in the form of Valerie, the new Section profiler. When the sexual competition commences, the two friends lash out at each other using technical and computer prowess and their age difference as darts. Birkoff redeems himself when he defends Walter's honor, ignorant of the fact that Walter has already moved on to greener and even younger pastures. Walter is definitely ready to earn Madeline's observation (in "Playing With Fire") that he is "a sixty-year-old teenager"!

T.J. Scott is ready to make full use of another one of Rocco Matteo's ever-creative club sets. Nikita in copper hair, a copper dress, sparkles, and lucite shoes enters the '60s/'70s plastic pop wonderland filled with transparent and peek-a-boo dance tubes, lit tubular tables, and retro furniture; distracting the bad guys with a little shimmy and shake.

"Third Party Ripoff" is also notable for its introduction of a substantial and, so far, likable secondary cast member, Davenport (played by Lawrence Bayne). Davenport, in the thankless role of Michael's replacement, is apologetic when Michael makes a rapid descent through the ranks to backup team. Davenport is an interesting choice for the job when you think about it: he is careful with Michael and doesn't make a fool of him in front of McDaniel (in the surprising alpha dog contest). He makes rather a soft play in the so-called "hard wedge," finally deferring to Michael mid-mission without ego or protest.

With the love scenes discreetly played out off-camera, the audience at least gets the bubble bath scene. Tenderness more than heat is evident as Nikita and Michael talk shop after a long day "at the office." The dramatic choice is intriguing, and it eventually pays off in the season's final scene.

Music

"Release" by **Afro Celt Sound System (with Sinead O'Connor/Iarla O'Lionaird)** on *Afro Celt Sound System: Vol. 2* (Real World) — club scene

Guest Cast

Lawrence Bayne (Davenport), Soo Garay (Valerie)

319 ANY MEANS NECESSARY

Written by Lawrence Hertzog
Directed by David Straiton

Birkoff is pulled from Com and sent into the field when he messes up during a mission because Hillinger has tampered with his communications systems. He intuits that his deep cover assignment with a cult-styled terrorist group, Soldats de la Liberté, will become permanent unless he can devise a way to get back to Section.

L — Gooderham and Worts Distillery
S — Birkoff's undercover apartment

L — Alley, west side of
#6 Adelaide Street East
S — "Dockside Bar"
(this location was also used for "Friend" during
the shootout scene where Nikita rescues Julie)

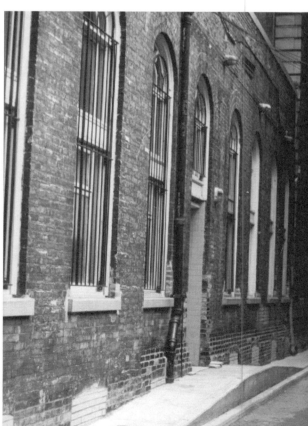

Matthew Ferguson really shines in this episode as he takes Birkoff on a voyage through hell. Under the pressures of fighting Hillinger on his own, Birkoff loses it big time. Strangely, he has isolated himself, not asking for Nikita's help in spite of all the help he's given her in the past. It seems Birkoff has a battlefield no less dangerous than the operatives'. Director David Straiton joins the series and makes a stylish debut here, particularly during Birkoff's "meltdown" scene. Straiton employs an effective and eerie technique, switching between video and film and using slow motion for just a couple of beats to convey Birkoff's disorientation.

Operations has been gunning for Birkoff since the beginning of the season but surely his reaction is overkill. Why would Operations put someone who knows Section's systems so intimately out in the field, so exposed? If Birkoff were to be turned after being abandoned by one father figure and "nurtured" by another, he would be a liability of the first order. Ironically, under better conditions the mission might have been tailor-made to Birkoff's skills.

Good blocking, as Birkoff brings Nikita up to speed from opposite doorways, emphasizes the lack of privacy in the fish bowl environment of Section. It also points out the adaptability of its inhabitants. Birkoff seems to understand absolute power, absolutely. He had no illusions about Michael when he took control of Section and here again he proves himself well able to process extreme scenarios, Section politics, and Operations' capriciousness.

The action sequence in the bar and even the phone call between Nikita and Birkoff contain some nice touches. Ferguson does a lot with his eyes. Birkoff telegraphs the ambush to Nikita with his eyes, giving her the split-second she needs to survive. When he phones her to set up the meeting he is wearing glasses to talk to Nikita, and he takes them off to talk to Rousseau. The move can be read as a cue to the audience to believe in Birkoff (one face for Nikita and one for Rousseau) and it can be read as remorse (Birkoff doesn't want to see himself in the mirror after he sets events in motion). The glasses also act as a tool to control Birkoff. Rousseau returns them like a gift when he's sure of Birkoff's compliance. Unfortunately, Jean-Marc Rousseau, the self-styled father figure and dapper, smooth villain, never proves particularly charismatic. Ferguson does all the work selling the question of whether or not Birkoff has gone over to the other side.

Lawrence Hertzog's last script of the season is an essay in how to fight a superior foe and survive — Birkie style. Birkoff is emerging as quite a dark horse this season, but his fair-play treatment of Hillinger is coming back to haunt him. It is fascinating to watch Birkoff map out the logic of how he has done his job and why he shouldn't be canceled. He has a faith in what he knows best: logic, literalism, and straight lines. He believes they will save him and they do, and he is able to match Operations move for move ("My orders were to get in and stay there . . . you gave the order to take me out, sir") like in a chess game. And he wins the game of semantics and logic, never once making an appeal to sentiment. Where Nikita or Walter would have argued fairness and humanity, Birkoff argues outcome and orders because at some level he puts his faith in the same things Operations does. The whole experience changes his sense of survival, as we will see.

Music

Original music by Sean Callery

Guest Cast

Kris Lemche (Hillinger), Andrew Gillies (Jean-Marc Rousseau), Colombe Demers (Mia), Christian Potenza (Reuben)

320 THREE-EYED TURTLE

Written by Maurice Hurley
Directed by Jon Cassar

Birkoff has finally learned his lesson: after covering for Hillinger's arrogant mistakes, he turns the boy genius in. While Nikita struggles to save Hillinger from certain death as an abeyance operative, Operations' abuse of Madeline peaks when George takes control of Section One's missions.

Writer Maurice Hurley takes the dark strains of sado-masochism that always bubble just beneath the surface in Section and plays them full volume right to the episode's end. After the horrifying escalation of humiliation, abuse, and harassment suffered by Madeline at the hands of Operations, we learn it's all been a ploy played to hidden cameras for the benefit of George. For the third time this season the writers have employed this same dramatic trick. One wonders just *where* all these cameras were and what kind of security Section really has if all these devices could have been planted with such ease. It feels like something of a cheat now and retrospectively casts a shadow over every conversation that's taken place within Section for the last two years.

The idea that Madeline is willing to betray Operations and make a power grab for herself seems so out of character (regardless of the abuse) that the audience gets the wink early and the fun lies, as always, in sitting back to watch who will get the upper hand. Watson and Glazer play it to the hilt in the public dressing-down, Madeline's submissive stance in committee, the cruel shot about her cheap smelling perfume, and the intensely distasteful post-coital discovery of a "branding" hickey. But it's a stalemate, for although Operations has been successful in securing the mysterious "Key File," he has also been promoting the very man who could bring him down by recovering the Gemstone File for George — Hillinger. Dressed in a dark suit instead of his usual teen gear, Hillinger looks every inch the

formidable enemy which he has actually been all along.

It remains a mystery why Birkoff continues to cover for Hillinger's obvious mistakes and why Nikita risks her life to save Hillinger's — now we know why the writers never drew Nikita into Birkoff's struggles. Hillinger's obvious maneuvering to be put in abeyance has seemed a bid for personal freedom, not Section betrayal. Matthew Ferguson is great here as Birkoff comes face to face with his own mortality in the van scene that could be his own post-trauma nightmare from "Noise." His contained show of anger in "Any Means Necessary" (in which he punches a wall and silently mouths a curse) now explodes publicly on his return to Section. Finally, he has the documented proof of Hillinger's manipulations that he's required all along — something tangible that Operations and Hillinger cannot explain away. It's a great moment when we see both Birkoff and Ferguson get to break out like that.

The political implications for Michael in all this upheaval are intriguing. His bargaining chip with Operations is gone now that George knows all about Adrian's death and Operations' power base. Although he scored points with George on the Bergomi mission, Operations' warning about blatantly choosing sides must be ringing in his ears. But until a victor emerges in this round of the "testosterone finals," he will have enough to keep him busy, as the next two episodes will show.

Music

Original music by Sean Callery

Guest Cast

Kris Lemche (Hillinger), David Hemblen (George), Alex Poch-Goldin (Rubin)

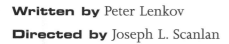

321 PLAYING WITH FIRE

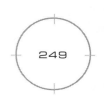

Written by Peter Lenkov
Directed by Joseph L. Scanlan

Madeline and Operations discover that Nikita and Michael are continuing their love affair in secret and devise a plan to end it. Mick Schtoppel asks for Nikita's help in impressing his mother, who is visiting from out of town.

Writer Peter Lenkov helms the two-part season finale which brings together Nikita and Michael only to have them torn apart in the cruelest of fashions. The heat between the lovers is finally more evident as Lenkov sets one of their trysts on the barge that was the scene of their first union. They play out the events of their second season reunion with Michael controlling the foreplay and Nikita (off-camera) submitting to another beating to cover their deception. Later, director of photography David Perrault bathes the duo in blue light creating an eyes-only visual feast for the pair. Although this is a beautiful sequence, set to the strains of David Sylvian's haunting voice, it goes on a little too long, giving it a disconcerting MTV touch.

Fresh from the fight of his life, Birkoff makes the understandable but still shocking move of ratting on Nikita and Michael *and* turning in Walter. Ferguson works hard to humanize the act with anger, discomfort, and regret but not even a concerned squeeze from Nikita's hand can dissuade him from self-preservation. Lawrence Bayne also returns as Davenport, whose membership in Walter's 5% club may be in question! Once again he is assigned the unpleasant task of bringing Michael down and his discomfort levels are apparent as he asks Operations to spell out just how far he is to go. The jury is still out on this character, who will be returning in the fourth season.

In a moment's reprieve from the claustrophobic Section, Mick Schtoppel (Carlo Rota) solicits Nikita's aid in impressing his mother with the lies of a marriage and a successful oral surgery practice. All

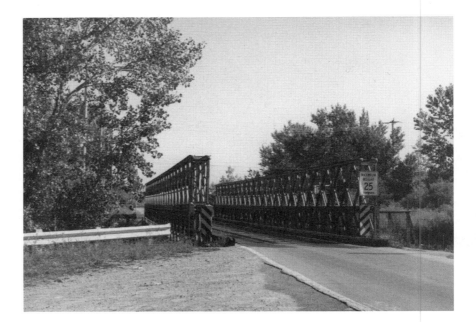

L — Unwin Avenue, west of Leslie Street
S — Michael loses Davenport

dressed up with nowhere to go, Mick gets the last minute blow-off from his mother, and we finally learn what all the needy kibitzing has been about. The scene establishes a nicely played connection between Nikita and her charge and even softened this viewer's hard heart.

In one of those "yes" moments Nikita, Michael, and Walter avoid the trap set by Operations and complete the Navaro mission. In a brilliant sequence, Madeline is the still center of a waiting game as Operations paces, Birkoff is worried and guilty, and Walter is disgusted. When the day is won, Birkoff and Walter exchange a flicker of pleasure and Don Francks shoots a classic Walter-styled "up yours" look to the aerie. Unfortunately, the victory will be short-lived.

Out from under the George-imposed magnifying glass it's business as usual with Operations and Madeline, who set about to determine and combat the level of threat Nikita and Michael's connection implies. The "hard wedge" has moved the relationship underground and added the allure of the forbidden, with stolen moments in back hallways and short but intense rendezvous. Once

L — Toronto Docks
S — "The Boat"

again Madeline and Operations create a self-fulfilling prophecy. By forbidding the relationship they drive it underground where it becomes covert and therefore suspect. For it to continue, Nikita and Michael seek and receive help from Walter, thus involving other operatives. The entire dynamic feeds their paranoia, be it a concern for security holes in the system or the fear of a power play by a duo that so far hasn't even conceived of such an act. It's Section in a nutshell and a view of the world through a self-reflecting lens.

Music

"Thalheim" by **David Sylvian** on *Dead Bees On A Cake* (EMI/Virgin) — Michael and Nikita gaze at one another

Guest Cast

Carlo Rota (Mick Schtoppel), Lawrence Bayne (Davenport)

322 ON BORROWED TIME

Written by Peter Lenkov
Directed by Ted Hanlan

Having convinced themselves that they've fooled Operations and Madeline, Nikita and Michael attempt to arrange time alone, but Madeline and Operations have devised a plan to get Walter out of the way so they can finally end the affair without any interference.

Desire seems to be clouding Nikita and Michael's judgment, for as soon as they are away on a mission Walter is sent to Retirement and Nikita is "adjusted." Michael's intuition might be acute enough to spot the Section agent at Genefex, but he completely misreads Operations' tolerance levels.

In the second part of the third season finale not one but two big questions, raised by Nikita as early as her arrival in Section, are addressed, though not entirely answered: Why hasn't she been canceled yet and what happens to older operatives who outlive their usefulness. Walter, the keeper of Section history, trivia, and gossip tells Birkoff that the prevailing myth is that Retirement is a hell of medical experiments, pain tolerance tests, and harvested body parts. That's one heck of a way to keep operatives motivated and productive! No doubt feeling more than his share of guilt over Walter's last close call, Birkoff assures Walter he will rescue him somehow. Birkoff seems to have overcome his fear of Operations, at least when it comes to saving Walter, because he enters the lion's den to enumerate the many reasons they should avoid doing "permanent" damage. Operations' amusement is understandable when Birkoff learns the whole exercise has been a test and a means to keep Walter out of the loop. Giles, Walter's replacement, is young, soft-spoken, bespectacled, and could pass for Birkoff's brother. But having sent Hillinger to abeyance and survived Operations plan to dispose of him, Birkoff is ready to sacrifice Giles if it means saving Walter. Quite a difference from the young man who cowered in his room begging Nikita not to kill him in "Noise."

The question of why Nikita is inside Section and why she has been allowed to live is addressed by Madeline immediately before she attempts to, at best, "adjust" or at worst remove the very quality Section claims to value in Nikita. There is something insane about Madeline's assertion that Section values Nikita's desire to "live life to the fullest" and something sad about her admission of envy. If we are to take George's word that Operations is devoid of emotion and accept Madeline's self-doubts from as early as "Gambit," then just what kind of monsters are these two? Human compassion and desire haven't been removed from their rule book; they weren't even factors in the equation to begin with.

Wilson and Dupuis end the season with one of the most painful scenes to date. Nikita in her white jacket, unkempt hair, 50-yard stare, and mindless painting looks like a candidate for the rubber room. What a difference from the angry, determined, and therapeutic apartment renovation of the second season. As though they've turned off a light, Madeline and Operations' "adjustment" seems to have taken root; Nikita has been re-made in their image as a hollow shell without feeling. Her repetition of "nothing" echoes like a Shakespearean tragedy. Feelings, desire, connection, and even her skin don't work. She and Michael have exchanged roles: he has virtually blossomed into a tender, compassionate man (at least with Nikita) and she has become a picture of Section efficiency, a "formidable operative" and that is all. Echoing Birkoff's pledge to Walter, Michael vows to rescue Nikita. After a year of loss — the loss of his son, the loss of his wife — it remains to be seen how Michael will deal with this new blow.

Music
"This Strange Effect" by **Hooverphonic** on *Blue Wonder Powder Milk* (Sony) — Michael and Nikita meet in a Section passageway

Guest Cast
Elias Zarou (Daimon Arrau), Andrew Kraulis (Giles), Steve Cumyn (Kellner)

SEVEN

SECTION-SPEAK

One of *La Femme Nikita*'s greatest achievements is the creative use of language by the writing team. Michael Loceff has been singled out as one of the team's great innovators, but viewers will agree that all the writers have made wonderful contributions to this major element of the series' overall style:

TERM	MEANING
5-year file	current collection of data (on a target) standardized to five years
a delta	a variance in a sample (chemical) from the norm
abeyance	an operative's status just prior to cancellation (expendable operatives are used for risky missions)
abort condition	events that require the cancellation of a mission
adjusted	euphemism given to chemical and electrical conditioning performed to control an operative's behavior
alpha secure	the highest level of communications or computer security
arbitrary	under suspicion

backstop	defensive position on a mission that protects the team's rear
baseline	standard against which a test can measure variance
bio trigger	trigger of a bomb planted within a person that uses the body's chemistry to activate it
black, the	death
black time	time that is not accounted for and is therefore suspicious
black track	a backup text record of events on a mission
blood cover	creation of a cover identity that is so realistic even a spouse and children don't know the reality
branch mission	a second mission plan connected to primary mission
breach	attack
buffered hostiles	isolated prisoners (who are kept ignorant of their captors' identities)
canceled	officially executed by Section
Casper Project	subliminal conditioning
cell	group or unit
class-five operative	a high ranking operative who reports directly to Operations (e.g., Michael)
class-one operative	entry-level operative who reports to a class-five operative
class-two operative	an operative who has been promoted and is no longer mentored by a class-five operative
clean (an area)	kill everyone
clock	cesium crystal implanted in operatives for tracking purposes
close quarters standby	condition whereby operatives remain inside Section awaiting a mission
cold op	seasoned or highly-trained operative in control of his emotions
collateral	incidental or expendable persons
com check	a check of communications
committee	physical area of Section used for meetings
compromised	discovered
condition blue	location is clear
conservative profile	behavior in the field that affords minimum interference

contained	controlled
containment	control (can be: bomb containment/personnel containment/situational containment)
critical mass	enough personnel to remain functional
dark	incommunicado
dark approach	protocol whereby operatives in the field sever electronic contact/communications with Section to preserve the safety of both
deep channel	communications channel outside standard frequencies used for covert or secure communication
def con scenario	defense condition situation (a term used in the Cold War that refers to levels of nuclear threat)
dirty zone	an area that is crawling with hostiles
disenfranchise	sever relationship with by extermination
disengage	distance oneself emotionally or physically
disposal	area inside Section where live explosives are safely detonated
drop out	an operative unable to complete a mission due to injury or disability
D.R.V.	Section department: Data Retrieval and Verification
E&A	egress and access
egress	exit route
endgame	final objective
exposure	visibility and therefore threat to secret status
field mechanics	mission skills
first team	team of operatives that leads the mission
flash mission	short notice protocol
gray	not according to mission plan
gray activity	criminally suspicious activity
green-list	list of protected or sanctioned criminals that Section uses for its own purposes
hard product	item manufactured from a design
hard wedge	an aggressive method of permanently separating two operatives who have become close
hostiles	bad guys
hot	live
housekeeping	Section "service" that removes corpses
in play	actively involved in a mission

incineration	complete destruction
incubate	isolate
innocents	civilians or those innocent of wrong-doing
insulate	isolate
intact	complete or whole
intel	data or information gathered
mandatory refusal	protocol whereby an agent protects the original mission plan in the event of a security breach by severing contact with Section
material secured	person or object captured
mode	appearance
non-operational profile	a record of what a person does in real life (and outside their criminal activities)
off profile	outside mission parameters
old life	life in the real world before Section
on mark	in position
operative	Section One agent
Oversight	ruling body that controls the Sections
peripheral activity	activity not directly involved with a mission
personnel configuration	placement of operatives at the site of a mission
P.O.S.	probability of survival (success)
preserved	kept alive
profile	pattern of mission activity
protocol	a convention, rule, or pattern
quiet filed	target or hostile presumed dead
recall	recollection of identity lost through a chemically induced amnesia
retirement	alternately describes the hell or paradise that awaits operatives past their prime
R.P.	retreat point
sanitize	kill everyone/remove all evidence of one's presence
saturate	overrun with operatives
scenario parameters	mission guidelines
secondary layer	secondary location or camp
segmentation condition	protocol whereby Section protects itself from the spread of contagion by isolating physical areas of Section
sequence anomaly	unforeseen or unplanned-for element that could

	interfere with a mission
sequencing	mission game plan
shadow profile	a second mission plan not connected to the primary mission
shadow recruitment	recruitment of someone with no criminal background who is pulled off the streets and framed by Section to ensure their cooperation
shadow team	secondary team attached to first team (without its knowledge and with a unique mission)
signature	uniquely identifiable features
sim	computer simulation
single	mission designed for one operative
singularity	one-time incident
sleeper	an agent-in-waiting (can be an individual pre-programmed to act out at the appropriate moment)
structural integrity	operational functionality
substation	secondary command center
surgical	extraction
sustained	survived
target terminated	person or object that is killed or destroyed
terminating	ending (can be a life, surveillance, etc.)
termination ranking	position on the list of abeyance operatives
Tower	secure rendezvous location for intimate encounters between Madeline and Operations
transferred	giving up information under torture or interrogation
Transit	mobile disposal unit
type-one directive	an irrevocable Section dictum
Valentine op	an operative that reels in his/her target through romantic or sexual manipulation
wet duplicate	a live, identical replacement
wet run	a low-risk mission that uses recruits for training purposes
Winchester Protocol	unknown protocol the use of which is forbidden by Oversight

LA FEMME NIKITA

Episodes by Director

Director	Writer	# Episode
Badiyi, Reza	Raskin, Larry	114 Recruit
	Janzen, Naomi	116 Missing
Bloomfield, George	Dettman, Andrew &	
	Truly, Daniel	108 Escape
	Loceff, Michael	110 Choice
	Loceff, Michael	112 Innocent
Bonnière, René	Hurley, Maurice	119 War
	Bellwood, Peter	121 Brainwashed
	Loceff, Michael	204 Approaching Zero
	Hurley, Maurice	208 Half Life
	Stern, Elliot	210 Open Heart
	Loceff, Michael	211 Psychic Pilgrim
	Loceff, Michael	216 Not Was
	Loceff, Michael	302 Someone Else's Shadow
	Cochran, Robert	304 Gates of Hell
	Loceff, Michael	311 Walk On By
	Hertzog, Lawrence	313 Beyond the Pale
Cassar, Jon	Nowrasteh, Cyrus	101 Nikita

EPISODE BY DIRECTOR

	Loceff, Michael	103 Love
	Loceff, Michael	113 Gambit
	Loceff, Michael	201 Hard Landing
	Loceff, Michael	203 Third Person
	Cochran, Robert	205 New Regime
	Cochran, Robert	217 Double Date
	Loceff, Michael	301 Looking for Michael
	Burke, David J.	303 Opening Night Jitters
	Hurley, Maurice	320 Three-Eyed Turtle
Ciccoritti, Jerry	Loceff, Michael	104 Simone
	Cochran, Robert	106 Treason
Fawcett, John	Ehrman, David	218 Off Profile
Giroitti, Ken	Cochran, Robert	109 Gray
	Bellwood, Peter	111 Rescue
	Ehrman, David	206 Mandatory Refusal
	Ehrman, David	207 Darkness Visible
	Loceff, Michael	213 Fuzzy Logic
	Hurley, Maurice	215 Inside Out
Hanlan, Ted	Hertzog, Lawrence	306 Love and Country
	Lenkov, Peter M.	322 On Borrowed Time (p.2)
Ingram, Terry	Hurley, Maurice	214 Old Habits
	Horowitz, Ed	307 Cat and Mouse
	Sloan, Michael	312 Threshold of Pain
	Loceff, Michael	316 I Remember Paris
	Horowitz, Ed	317 All Good Things
Jacobson, Rick	Lenkov, Peter M.	309 Slipping into Darkness
	Lenkov, Peter M.	310 Under the Influence
Johnson, Clark	Cochran, Robert	219 Last Night
Langevin, Gord	Korris, Jim	308 Outside the Box
Magar, Guy	Janzen, Naomi	105 Friend
	Janzen, Naomi	107 Mother
	Mohan, Peter & Henshaw, Jim	209 First Mission
Scanlan, Joseph L.	Loceff, Michael	122 Mercy
	Loceff, Michael	220 In Between
	Cochran, Robert & Ehrman, David	222 End Game

NINE

LA FEMME NIKITA

Episodes by Writer

Writer	Director	# Episode
Bellwood, Peter	Giroitti, Ken	111 Rescue
	Bonnière, René	121 Brainwashed
Burke, David J.	Cassar, Jon	303 Opening Night Jitters
Cochran, Robert	Skogland, Kari	102 Charity
	Ciccoritti, Jerry	106 Treason
	Giroitti, Ken	109 Gray
	Scott, T.J.	115 Obsessed
	Shilton, Gilbert	120 Verdict
	Scott, T.J.	202 Spec Ops
	Cassar, Jon	205 New Regime
	Cassar, Jon	217 Double Date
	Johnson, Clark	219 Last Night
	Bonnière, René	304 Gates of Hell
Cochran, Robert & Ehrman, David	Scanlan, Joseph L.	222 End Game
Dettman, Andrew & Truly, Daniel	Bloomfield, George	108 Escape
Ehrman, David	Giroitti, Ken	206 Mandatory Refusal

EPISODE BY WRITER

SOURCES

Newspapers and Magazines

Abraham, Carolyn. "Hollywood North: Toronto." *Ottawa Citizen.* June 23, 1997.

Adair, Connie. "You Oughta Be in Pictures." *Toronto Star.* Feb. 21, 1999. p. E1.

Adilman, Sid. "'Quebec Brando' Follows Instincts." *Toronto Star.* June 26, 1994. p. B11.

Advertisements. *Entertainment Weekly.* Mar. 19, 1999. p. 35, 37, 39.

"Arielle Dombasle Revives Roy Dupuis' Virility!" *La Presse* July 6, 1996.

"Armed & Dangerous." *Shape.* August 1998. p. 116–121.

Barker, Angela, et al. "Nikita." *TV Guide* (Canada). Jan. 16, 1999. p. 6.

Bawden, Jim. "Nikita's Iciest Femme Fatale." *Toronto Star.* July 18, 1999. p. D22.

Beaumanis, Viia. "Peta Wilson." *Flare.* March, 1999. Cover, 106–115.

Beck, Marilyn, et al. "Femme Fatale, or Maybe Not?" *San Jose Mercury News.* Jan. 13, 1999.

Beland, Nicole, et al. "12 Women Who Rocked Our Year." *Cosmopolitan.* February 1998. p. 138.

"Benefit for Midwives: Feb. 26." *Montreal Gazette.* Feb. 21, 1990.

Bennett, Alysia. "Peta Wilson, TV Commando." *Washington Post.* December 1998.

Bernard, April P. "Armed and Dangerous." *Seventeen.* July 1997. p. 88.

Bernstein, Jonathan. "Cherchez la
Femme." *Gear.* Sept./Oct. 1998.
p. 13, 72–79, cover.

Bickley, Claire. "Crewson on a Role."
Toronto Sun. Oct. 17, 1998.

___. "The Beauty and the Brains."
Toronto Sun. Feb. 24, 1997.

Bowles, Jennifer . "Transforming
Nikita." *Standard–Times.* Feb. 3,
1997.

Braun, Liz. "Happy in Her Work."
Toronto Sun. Dec. 29, 1995.

Brioux, Bill. "Femme Fatale." *TV Guide*
(Canada). Apr. 12–18, 1997.
p. 24–25.

Brioux, Bill. "Still on Display." *TV
Guide* (Canada). Nov. 19, 1994.
p. 16–20.

Brockway, Laurie Sue. "La Femme
Nikita's Roy Dupuis." *Single Living.*
Sept./Oct. 1997.

Brown, Ross. "She's a Killer Queen."
FHM. May 1999. p. 92–93, 95.

Brownstein, Bill. "Roy Dupuis's Train
Has Come In." *Montreal Gazette.*
Nov. 29, 1993. p. F5, F6.

Came, Barry. "The Dionne Quint-
Essence." *Macleans.* June 6, 1994.
p. 92–94.

Carson, Tom. "La Femme Dilbert."
Village Voice. Jan. 13, 1998. p. 77.

Che, Cathay. "Who's L'Homme?"
Time Out (NY). Mar. 26–Apr. 2,
1998.

Chun, Rene. "Her Way Tomorrow's
Tastemakers." *In Style.* May 1997.

Chun, Rene. "Her Way: Peta Wilson."
In Style. August 1997.

Chun, Rene, et al. "Style Guide." *In
Style.* September 1997.
p. 206–220.

Clarke, Steve. "Euro Trip to Market
Fills Local Programming Holes."
Variety. Jan 12–18, 1998. p. 148.

Coleman, Lisa. "Peta Wilson talks to
Prevue." *Prevue.* January 1999.

Crew, Robert. "Le Chien's English
Debut and Underwhelming
Event." *Toronto Star.* Nov. 18,
1988.

"Cybertalk: The Dead Zone."
Entertainment Weekly. Aug. 1, 1997.
p. 81.

Daignault, Daniel. "Roy Dupuis: Sa
Vie a Change." *Echo Vedettes.*
Mar. 13, 1999.

Dempsey, John. "USA's 'Nikita,' 'Rudy'
on $175 Million Roster." *Variety.*
Apr. 29–May 5, 1996. p. 40.

___. "Femme Leads Earn Piece of the
Action." *Variety.* July 14–20,
1997. p. 25, 28.

Donnelly, Pat. "Powerful Acting Lifts
Un Oiseau." *Montreal Gazette.* Jan.
21, 1990.

Doonan, Simon, et al. "Best & Worst
Dressed '98." *People.*
Sept. 14, 1998. p. 126.

"Elementary, Watson." *Detour.* May
1996.

Elle Quebec. March 1992.

Endrst, James. "Nikita Shoots Down
Under." *Toronto Star.* Aug. 19,
1997. p. E4.

"The Eyes Have It In Engrossing Nikita." *Denver Rocky Mountain News* Jan. 3, 1999.

"Falling in Love is a Gift." *7 Jours.* Sept. 3, 1994.

"Fantastic 4: La Femme Nikita — Peta Wilson." *Celebrity Sleuth Women of Fantasy* #9 Vol. 11, Issue 6. 1998. p. 8–11.

Flint, Joe. "USA Books 'Brooks' on Prep Sked." *Variety.* July 17–23, 1995. p. 25.

____. "On The Air." *Entertainment Weekly.* Aug. 1, 1997. p. 54.

Forman, Gayle. "La Femme Peta." *Seventeen.* August 1998. p. 182, 185.

"French Films, American Accents." *Economist.* Feb. 27, 1993. p. 89.

"Getting the Heroine Habit." *Sydney Morning Herald.* July 30, 1997.

Gliatto, Tom. "Picks & Pans: La Femme Nikita." *People.* Feb. 3, 1997. p. 15.

Goodale, Gloria. "Television's Superwomen." *Christian Science Monitor.* Feb. 5, 1999.

Goodman, Tim. "Femme Fatale." *TV Guide* (*Sunday Telegraph* [Australia]). Dec. 6, 1998.

Graham, Jefferson. "Nikita Star Wilson is Cable's Hit Woman." *USA Today.* July 29, 1999.

Gray, Ellen. "Some TV Guys You'd Want on Your Side." *Toronto Star.* Dec. 3, 1997. p. F4.

Grisoli, Mimi. "La Femme Nikita: Not Just Another Pretty Face." *Driftwood Newspaper.* Mar. 6, 1997.

____. "La Femme Nikita: Not Just Another Pretty Face." *Driftwood On Shore.* Mar. 6, 1997.

Gross, Edward. "French Twist." *Cinescape.* July 1996. p. 42–45.

____. "The Peta Principle." *Femmes Fatales.* Apr. 16, 1999. p. 24–29.

Hamel, Francois. Nikita Special Issue. *7 Jours.* Aug. 28, 1999. cover, p. 8–19.

____. "Roy Dupuis." *Le Lundi.* May 22, 1999.

"Hemoglobin Review." *Empire.* March 1998.

Hobson, Louis B. "Scream(er) Therapy." *Edmonton Sun.* Jan. 29, 1996.

"Home Sweet Home." *Le Lundi* Mar. 20, 1999.

"Homme de Reves." *Elle Quebec.* February 1996. p. 20–22.

Hontz, Jenny. "Nikita's Surnow Pacts with WBTV." *Variety.* July 22, 1998.

"I Had Problems With Anorexia." *7 Jours.* May 22, 1999.

"Inside Scoop." *Who Weekly.* December, 1998.

"Interview with Marina Orsini." *7 Jours.* Dec. 4, 1993.

Irmler, Meghan. "Scene+heard: Conquering Cortes." *In Style.* September 1998. p. 182.

"It's the Year of TV Tough Girl — Now, Nikita." *Virginian-Pilot.* 1997.

James, Caryn. "Hit Man: Stylish Deadly Female." *New York Times.* Jan. 13, 1997. p. C15.

Jicha, Tom. "Action, Flesh — 'Nikita' is Back." Knight-Ridder News Service. Jan. 6, 1997.

Johnson, Brian. "Sexual Wildlife." *Macleans*. Nov. 9, 1992. p. 108.

Johnson, Eric. "The Tubular Belle." *Metro Santa Cruz*. Sept. 18–24, 1997.

Kaltenbach, Chris. "'Nikita' Knocks 'em Dead." *SunSpot TV (Baltimore Sun)*. Sept. 10, 1997.

Kaltman, Naomi. "24-Hour Style." *Redbook*. July 1999. p. 80–85.

Karlin, Beth. "Style Watch: Puff Pieces." *People*. Mar. 2, 1998. p. 91.

Kelly, Brendan. "Show Biz Chez Nous." *Montreal Gazette*. June 16, 1997. p. C5.

____. "With Nikita, The Earth Moved." *Montreal Gazette*. May 1, 1999.

Kelly, Janet. "Actress is the Cat's Meow." *Cambridge Reporter*. Nov. 5, 1998. p. 3.

King, Susan. "Don't Cry for TV's Nikita: She's a Hit." *LA Times*. Aug. 1, 1997.

____. "Oui, Nikita." *LA Times*. Aug. 3, 1997.

Kittenplan, Susan. "TV's Girl Power." *Harper's Bazaar*. September 1998. p. 511.

Kushman, Rick. "Comedy Reigns on Fox's Hill." *Sacramento Bee*. Jan. 11, 1997.

Landry, Gabriel. "Roy Dupuis." 24 *Images*. Feb./Mar. 1993. p. 12–13.

Lang, Steven. "Femme Fatale." *People*. Apr. 4 or 14, 1997. p. 67.

Laurence, Kel. "La Femme Peta Wilson." *Ralph*. March 1999. cover, p. 32–37.

Leiren-Young, Mark. "One on One With La Femme Nikita." *TV Week*. May 23, 1998.

Littlefield, Kinney. "Woman Power Results in She Shorts." *Edmonton Journal*. Aug. 3, 1998. p. C4.

Lorando, Mark. "Femme Nikita Star Savors Success." *Seattle Times*. Mar. 27, 1998.

"Love is More Important Than Marriage." *Katso*. Mar. 13, 1999.

Le Lundi. June 19, 1992.

Macdonald, Ron Foley, et al. "From Sea To Sea (Movie Making In Canada)." *Take One*. Spring 1997. p. 40–42.

Matthews, Regina. "Hot Fun in the Summertime." *CableWorld*. Sept. 1, 1997.

McConville, Jim. "Charting Last Season's Original Hits and Misses." *Electronic Media*. Sept. 29, 1997. p. 43.

McKay, John. "New Blood." *Montreal Gazette*. Sept. 14, 1996. p. E3.

McLeod, Tyler. "Crewson's Haunting Role." *Calgary Sun*. Jan. 22, 1999.

Menon, Vinay. "Entertainment Brokers Hit Fertile Ground Running." *Toronto Star*. May 24, 1998. p. D1.

Miller, Sarah. "8 Babes a Week." *Details*. October 1997. p. 148–155.

Morton, Neil. "In Praise of Alberta Watson." *Elm Street.* May 1998. p. 22–31.

"My New Lifestyle." *7 Jours.* Dec. 7, 1996.

"Nikita Makes Killing With Fans." *Lexington Herald-Leader.* Aug. 1, 1997.

Parish Perkins, Ken. "They Barely Dress for TV Success." Knight-Ridder News Service. July 25, 1997.

Perkins, Ken Parish. "Peta Kicks "Nikita" Up a Notch From Its Film Original." *Star-Telegram.com.* Jan. 2, 1999.

"Peta Makes a Killing." *New Weekly.* Dec. 14, 1998.

"Peta Wilson #2." *Celebrity Sleuth: 25 Sexiest Women of 1999.* Vol. 12, Issue 3. 1999. p. 90–93.

Philip, John. "Peta the Great." GQ (Australia). Dec./Jan. 1998.

Playboy. July 1998.

Potter, Mitch. "Toronto, You're On." *Toronto Star.* Oct. 18, 1998.

La Presse. Sept. 19, 1994.

La Presse. Jan. 8, 1994.

Le Presse. Feb. 29, 1992.

"Quebec Actor Breaking Into Quebec Cinema." Canadian Press Newswire. Sept. 11, 1996.

"Quebec's Hottest Actor." CP. *Toronto Star.* Aug. 6, 1992. p. C8.

Quinones, Eric R. "Bob Guccione Jr. Takes Another Shot at Magazine." Associated Press. Aug. 12, 1998.

Rettenmund, Matthew, ed. "L'Homme de La Femme Nikita." *Hollywood's Hottest Hunks #2.* June 15, 1998. p. 94.

"Return of the Prodigal Son." *Le Devoir* Oct. 21, 1995.

Rioux, Christian. "En Plein Vol." *L'actualite.* August 1993. p. 22–27, cover.

Rochlin, Margy. "Taking 13 Hours to Fix the Errors Made in 90 Minutes." *New York Times.* Jan. 10, 1999.

"Roy and Sime." *7 Jours.* Mar. 28, 1992.

"Roy Dupuis." *Hollywood's Hottest Hunks* (Bio-Pix). Vol. 3, Issue 2. 1999. p. 61.

"Roy Dupuis . . . Avec Claude." *La Presse.* Feb. 1, 1992.

"Roy Dupuis in an American Series." *La Presse.* Mar. 16, 1994.

"Roy Dupuis in Being At Home With Claude." *Le Soleil.* Feb. 20, 1992.

"Roy Dupuis: Interview." *7 Jours.* Sept. 30, 1995.

"Roy Dupuis: La Belle Bete." *Elle Quebec.* November 1993. p. 30–33.

"Roy Dupuis' New Life." *7 Jours.* Mar. 20, 1999.

"Roy Dupuis Renoue Avec Le Theatre." *Video-Presse.* December 1993. p. 20–22.

"Roy Dupuis: The American Dream." *7 Jours.* May 1997.

"Roy Dupuis: The Wildman Is

Tamed." *Chatelaine* (French). August 1991.

Rubin, Sylvia. "The New Femme Fatale." *San Francisco Chronicle.* Sept. 17, 1997.

Ryan, Kimberley. "Talking Fashion." *Vanity Fair.* September 1998. p. 224.

Scapperotta, Dan. "*La Femme Nikita.*" *Femmes Fatales.* August 1997.

Seal, Mark. "Roy Dupuis' Montreal." *American Way.* February 1998.

Seguin, Denis. "Quaint Quebec." *Eye.* Mar. 20, 1997.

Shih, Julia. "Sexy Nikita Makes Waves for USA." *Michigan Daily Online.* Apr. 7, 1997.

Snierson, Dan. "La Femme Peta." *Entertainment Weekly.* Aug. 1, 1997. p. 34.

Sterne, Hilary. "Hot Zone: Peta Wilson." *Us Magazine.* June 1997. p. 43.

Stone, Sally. "Wilson Seen as the Mrs. Peel of the 90's." *Spokane.Net.* June 3, 1998.

Storey, Michael. "Nikita Star Down-to-Earth." *Little Rock Newspapers.* Nov. 6, 1997.

Stoynoff, Natasha. "A Sweet Start." *Toronto Sun.* Sept. 5, 1997. p. 61.

____. "Nikita Ready for Action." *Toronto Sun.* Mar. 2, 1997.

Sullivan, Robert. "Peta's Time-Killer Workout." *Women's Sports & Fitness.* Nov./Dec. 1998. p. 130–133.

Swallow, Jim. "*La Femme Nikita.*" *Cult TV* January 1998.

Tannenbaum, Rob. "Peta Wilson." *Details.* August 1997. p. 122–123.

"The Tender Face of Roy Dupuis." *Tele Indiscreta.* Mar. 6, 1999.

"There's a Plentiful Supply." *Le Soleil.* July 22, 1996.

Toth, Kathleen. "Cherchez La Femme." *Dreamwatch.* November 1997.

Tume, Grant. "Une Femme Dangereuse." *Detour.* Dec./Jan. 1998. p. 72–73, poster.

Ventura, Michael. "Warrior Women." *Psychology Today.* Nov./Dec. 1998. p. 58.

"La Vie de Famille de Roy Dupuis." *7 Jours* Jan. 13, 1996.

"What's For Sale at MIP." *Variety* Apr 7–13, 1997. p. 94.

Wickens, Barbara, ed. "Boss To A Lethal Babe." *Macleans.* Apr. 28, 1997. p. 54.

Witmer, Eli. "Three Popular Action Guys." *Toronto Star.* Sept. 28, 1997. p. TV5.

Wyatt, Nelson. "Quebec Actor Learning To Handle Fame." *Calgary Herald* Aug. 7, 1992. p. C10.

"Yellowknife Mine Tragedy Focus of New CBC Movie." Canadian Press Newswire. Dec. 3, 1996.

Yovanovich, Linda. *Cable TV Magazine.*

Zekas, Rita. "Now Kidder Pedals her Butt all Over Town." *Toronto Star.* July 23 1999. p. D4.

Zutell, Irene. "Raiders of the Big Screen." *People.* Mar. 31, 1997. p. 19.

Online Articles

"Alberta Watson." Chat Transcript. *TV Guide Online*. Jan. 7, 1999.
   www.tvguide.com/chat/transcripts/ts010799aw.asp

Anderson, Porter. "*La Femme Nikita*: Pain Perfect." CNN *Interactive*. Aug. 6, 1999.
   cnn.com/SHOWBIZ/TV/9908/06/nikita.season3/

Baerg, Greg. "A Brand New Season of Nikita." *UltimateTV*. Jan. 2, 1999.
   www.ultimatetv.com/news/f/a/99/01/02nikita.html

"BBS Transcript: Peta Wilson." Chat Transcript. *TV Guide Online*. June 30, 1997.
   www.tvgen.com/bbs/transcripts/peta.htm

Bianculli, David. "'Femme' May Be Fatale to Her Masters." *New York Daily
   News Online*. Aug. 21, 1998.
   www.nydailynews.com/1998-08-21/New_York_Now/Television/
   a-2947.asp

"BIO — Peta Wilson." *UltimateTV*
   www.ultimatetv.com/news/b/w/petawilson.html

"Bob Cochran." WB *Virtual Lot Presents: Cybertalk!* Aug. 31, 1998.
   www.lafemmenikita.com/cmp/original/transbc.htm

"Cable Ace Awards: Peta Wilson & Evander Holyfield." Etonline. 1997.
   www.etonline.com/html/ChatSchedule/71.html

"Chat: Roy Dupuis." *UltimateTV*.
   www.ultimatetv.com/promolounge/bts/usa/lafemmenikita/

Cochran, Beth E. "Peta Wilson." *2upbeatmag.com*.
   www.2upbeatmag.com/peta.htm

Cooper, Gina Pia, ed. "Laurie Drew." *FashionFinds.com*. April 1999.
   http://www.fashionfinds.com

____, ed. "Roy Dupuis: The Actor's Method." *FashionFinds.com*. July 1999.
   www.fashionfinds.com/july/pages/roy-dupuis-1.html

"Daily News: Perth Resigns From USA." *UltimateTV*. June 10, 1998.
   www.ultimatetv.com/news/h/98/6/980610daily.html

Decker, Shelly. "Effects Just Aren't Special." JAM! Aug. 28, 1998.
   www.canoe.ca/JamMoviesReviewsO/oneofourown_decker.html

____. "One Of Our Own." JAM! Aug. 28, 1998.
   www.canoe.ca/JamMoviesArtistsH/harvey_bruce.html

"Don Francks." Chat Transcript. *TV Guide Online*. Jan. 8, 1999.

http://www.tvguide.com/chat/transcripts/ts010899df.asp

Dunlevy, Dagmar. "Peta Wilson." *The Dag-Star.* 1999.
  www.celebritysightings.com/mz-dagstar01.cfm

Ehrman, David. "Q&A: Ehrman." *Nikita.com.* 1998.
  www.nikita.com/cmp/original/qanda2.htm

Entertainment Weekly Online. Mar. 7, 1997.
  cgi.pathfinder.com/ew/970307/features/xena/xena2.html
  (no longer on site)

Entertainment Weekly Online. Aug. 1, 1997.
  cgi.pathfinder.com/ew/970801/multimedia/mm-cyberta
  (no longer on site)

"Eugene Robert Glazer." Chat Transcript. *TV Guide Online.* Jan. 6, 1999.
  http://www.tvguide.com/chat/transcripts/ts010699eg.asp

"Eugene Robert Glazer." *AOL's Entertainment.* Summer 1998. Stored:
  ljc.simplenet.com/nikita/gene_asylum.html

"Eugene Robert Glazer." *WB Virtual Lot Presents: Cybertalk!* July 24, 1997.
  www.lafemmenikita.com/cmp/original/transerg.htm

"Fact Sheet — Peta Wilson." *E!Online.* 1999.
  www.eonline.com/Facts/People/Bio/0,128,49657,00.html

Fagan, Greg. "Nikita: A Killer's Site." *TV Guide Online.* Mar. 23, 1998.
  www.tvgen.com/tv/magazine/980323/web.htm

Feldman, Len P. "La Femme Peta Wilson." *Gist.com.* Aug. 27, 1997.
  www.gist.com/tv/drama/archive_ap.dpg?adf=dr082797

"*La Femme Nikita* Debuts Internationally." *Time Warner Report.* December.
  www.pathfinder.com/corp/tvreport/1997/december/
  (no longer on site)

"*Femme Nikita* Favorites Announced." *UltimateTV* Jan. 27, 1999.
  www.ultimatetv.com/news/h/99/01/TVNewsDaily_043.ht

Goodwin, Betty. "Screen Style: *La Femme Nikita*." *UltimateTV.* Oct. 23, 1997.
  www.ultimatetv.com/news/f/a/97/10/23nikita.htm

"Gossip: Star Boards — Peta Wilson." *E!Online.* 1999.
  www.eonline.com/Gossip/Star/Wilson

Green, Michelle Erica. "*La Femme Nikita* on Strength, Stamina & Role
  Model." *AnotherUniverse.com.* May 1998.
  www.anotheruniverse.com/tv/features/petawilsonnikita.html

____. "Kings, Queens, Knights, Pawns." *AnotherUniverse.com.* September 1998.

www.anotheruniverse.com/tv/features/lafemmenikitaseason.html

___. "Toughest Woman on Television." *AnotherUniverse.com*. December 1998.
www.anotheruniverse.com/tv/features/albertawatson.html

Greene, Penelope. "In the Belly of the Fashion Publicity Beast." *New York Times Online*. September 1999.
www.nytimes.com

Gross, Edward. "La Femme Fatale." *Retrovisionmag.com*.
www.retrovisionmag.com/la_femme_fatale.htm

___. "Undercover Blues." *Retrovisionmag.com*.
www.retrovisionmag.com/la_femme_fatale.htm

"Joel Surnow." Chat Transcript. *TV Guide Online*. Aug. 20, 1999.
www.tvguide.com/chat/transcripts/ts082099JS.asp

"Joel Surnow, Peta Wilson, Roy Dupuis." *Universal Studios: The Backlot Café*. Mar. 31, 1998.
www.fortunecity.com/victorian/literary/216/chat.html

"Joel Surnow, Peta Wilson, Roy Dupuis." *WB Virtual Lot Presents: Cybertalk!* February 1998.

Kelly, Ron ,ed. "Wired: Peta Project." *Total TV*. Jan. 3, 1998.
www.tottv.com/i980103/wired.html (Total TV is no longer online.)

Kitman, Marvin. "The Marvys." *UltimateTV* Aug. 28, 1997.
www.ultimatetv.com/news/columns/kitman/970829kitman

Kitman, Marvin. "Time for House Cleaning at the TV Academy." *UltimateTV*. Aug. 7, 1997.
www.ultimatetv.com/news/columns/kitman/970807kitman

"Laurie Drew." *Live Chat* LFN Con. Oct. 3, 1998.
www.lafemmenikita.com/cmp/original/transld.htm

Loceff, Michael. "LAQ — Loceffian Answered Questions." LFN *Usenet*. Feb. 5, 1998. posted to newsgroups in answer to fan questions

___. "Q&A: Loceff." *Nikita.com*. 1998.
www.nikita.com/cmp/original/q-a204.htm

"Loser." *Loser Web Site*. 1996. www.filmkitchen.com/loser/

Lyons, Shelly. "The Brecht Girl." *UltimateTV*. Jan. 2, 1998.
www.ultimatetv.com/news/f/a/98/01/02nikita.html

Martindale, David. "Peta Wilson: Nikita is Quite a Hit, Lady." *UltimateTV*. Aug. 20, 1999. www.ultimatetv.com/Features.html?3178

Martinez, Jose A. "The Femme Mystique." *TV Guide Online*. Oct. 4, 1997.

SOURCES

www.tvgen.com/tv/magazine/970929/insider3.htm

"Matthew Ferguson." Chat Transcript. *TV Guide Online*. Jan. 4, 1999.
    http://www.tvguide.com/chat/transcripts/ts010499mf.asp

McDonald, Stef. "Love and Death." *TV Guide Online*. Mar. 7, 1998.
    www.tvgen.com/

____. "Peta's Principles." *TV Guide Online*. June 9, 1997.
    www.tvgen.com/tv/magazine/970609/ftr4a.sml

McEntire, Torri. "Nikita Is." *UltimateTV*. Jan. 24, 1997.
    www.ultimatetv.com/news/r/a/97/01/24nikita.html

McLeod, Tyler. "Peta's Big Chill." *JAM!* Jan. 29, 1999.
    www.canoe.ca/TelevisionShowsL2Q/nikita.html

____. "Predictable Cop Drama Skimps on Peta." *JAM!*. Aug. 28, 1998.
    www.canoe.ca/JamMoviesReviewsO/oneofourown_ mcleod.html

Miller, Kirk. "Hot Faces '97: Peta Wilson." *Total TV*. July 26, 1997.
    www.tottv.com/i970726/feature1.html

Millman, Joyce. "1997: The Year in Television." *Salon.com*. December 1997.
    www.salon1999.com/ent/tv/1997/12/24best.html

Nielson, Dave. "Losing It With Peta." *AOL's Entertainment Asylum*. Summer
    1998.

O'Shea, Tara. "K. Douglas Macrae." *LJC Exclusive Interviews*. 1998.
    ljc.simplenet.com/nikita/doug_interview.html

____. "Lawrence Hertzog." *LJC Exclusive Interviews*. 1999.
    ljc.simplenet.com/nikita/larry_interview.html

____. "Matthew Ferguson." *LJC Exclusive Interviews*. 1998.
    ljc.simplenet.com/nikita/matthew_interview.html

____. "She's No Girl From U.N.C.L.E." *Total TV*. 1998.
    www.totaltv.com/topten/nikita/t10nikita.html

____. "Tara Sloane." *LJC Exclusive Interviews*. 1998.
    ljc.simplenet.com/nikita/tara_interview.html

"Passages des Hommes Libres." *Telefilm Canada Online*. 1997.
    www.telefilm.gc.ca/en/prod/film/film96/20.htm

Peck, Michael. "Peta Wilson: A Face That Stops Traffic." *TV Guide Online*. July
    13, 1998. www.tvgen.com

"Peta Wilson." Chat Transcript. *TV Guide Online*. Jan. 5, 1999.
    http://www.tvguide.com/chat/transcripts/ts010599pw.asp

"Peta Wilson." Chat Transcript. *TV Guide Online*. Mar. 30, 1998. www.tvgen.com

"Peta Wilson." *Sexy Women Celebrities*. 1997.

www.kcweb.com/super/p_wilson.htm

"Q&A with *La Femme Nikita's* Peta Wilson." *UltimateTV.* Mar. 20, 1997. www.ultimatetv.com/news/f/a/97/03/20peta.html

Roush, Matt. "The Roush Review: *La Femme Nikita.*" *TV Guide Online.* Mar. 23, 1998. www.tvgen.com/tv/magazine/980323/roush.htm (The TV Guide is www.tvguide.com and no longer archives its older material.)

"Roy Dupuis." *BoxTop Live Chat.* February 1998. www.universalstudios.com

"Roy Dupuis." Chat Transcript. *TV Guide Online.* Jan. 3, 1999. http://www.tvguide.com/chat/transcripts/ts010399rd.asp

"Roy Dupuis." Chat Transcript. *UltimateTV.* February 1998. www.ultimatetv.com/interact/live/roy_dupuis/page1.html

Rudolph, Ileane, and Lynn Rudolph. "Real A-Peel." *TV Guide Online.* May 10, 1997. www.tvgen.com

Sellers, John. "Violent Femme." *MrShowbiz.com.* April 1998. mrshowbiz.go.com/interviews/410_1.html

"10 Best-Dressed Stars on TV: Peta Wilson #3." *TV Guide Online.* Aug. 9, 1997. www.tvgen.com

Transcript. "Chat Transcript: Mark Snow." *TV Guide Online.* June 16, 1998. www.tvgen.com/chat/transcripts/ts061698ms.html

Walsh, John. "On the Go With Peta Wilson." *TV Guide Online.* Jan. 15, 1999. www.tvgen.com

Walsh, John. "What a Relief." *TV Guide Online.* Summer?? 1998. www.tvgen.com

"You Sexy Thing!" *TV Guide Online.* Aug. 17, 1998. www.tvguide.com/features/yst/990817/

Nikita TV

Peta Wilson. *Canada AM* (CTV). Mar. 11, 1998.

Peta Wilson. *Danny Bonaduce Show.* June 5, 1998.

Roy Dupuis and Peta Wilson. *Entertainment Television.* May 29, 1997.

Roy's Interview. *Entertainment Tonight.* May 26, 1997.

Peta Wilson. *Fox Entertainment.* June 5, 1998.

Peta Wilson, Don Francks, and Eugene Robert Glazer. *Jane Hawtin Live.* May 20, 1998.

Peta Wilson. *Late Night with Conan O'Brien.* 1997.

Peta Wilson. *Late Show with David Letterman.* 1998.

Peta Wilson. *Live with Regis and Kathie Lee.* 1997.

Peta Wilson. *On the Arts* (CBC). 1997.

Alberta Watson. *Open Mike with Mike Bullard.* Nov. 24, 1998.

Peta Wilson. *Politically Incorrect.* June 12, 1998.

Peta Wilson. *Politically Incorrect.* Feb. 22, 1999.

Peta Wilson. *Rosie O'Donnell.* Mar. 13, 1998.

Peta Wilson. *Rosie O'Donnell.* Mar. 31, 1997.

Peta Wilson. *Tonight With Jay Leno.* May 30, 1997.

Matthew Ferguson. USA Network:USA *Open Chat.* Sept. 4, 1998.

Books

Rocklin *Celebrity Directory.* 9th ed. Ann Arbor: Axiom Information Resources, 1999. (Subject Peta Wilson)

Contemporary Theatre, Film and Television. Detroit-London: Gale, 1999. (Subject Peta Wilson)

Contemporary Theatre, Film and Television. Detroit-London: Gale, 1999. (Subject Roy Dupuis)

Face To Face with Talent. Toronto : The Association, 1993–94. (Subject Matthew Ferguson)

La Femme Nikita X-Posed. Rocklin, CA: Prima Publishing, 1998.

PHOTO CREDITS

Front cover: James Minchin/Outline

Back cover: Yoram Kahana/Shooting Star

Black and white glossy photo section: Courtesy Claire Burton

Color section, in order: James Minchin/Outline; Theo Kingma/ Shooting Star; *The Gazette*, Montreal; Andrew Eccles/Outline; James Minchin/Outline; Close Quarters Standby; Close Quarters Standby; Andrew Eccles/Outline; Sonia Moskowitz/Globe Photos; R. Madonik/*Toronto Star*; Daniela Stallinger; Nancy Kaszerman/Zuma Press; Christopher Little/Outline; Arnaldo Magnani/Gamma-Liaison; *The Gazette*, Montreal; Daniela Stallinger

Black and white photos in text: Photos courtesy Peggy Sinclair: 3, 4, 5, 7, 10

Copyright Russ Einhorn/Gamma-Liaison: 15

Copyright Christopher Little/Outline: 25

Photos courtesy Kodak Canada/Narvali: 27, 81, 120, 122

Photos courtesy *The Gazette*, Montreal: 36

Photos courtesy Close Quarters Standby: 43, 44, 45, 68, 70, 72, 74, 77, 78, 80, 85, 86, 224

Copyright Paul Fenton/Globe Photos: 48

Copyright Globe Photos: 50

Photos courtesy Dawn Connolly: 76, 91, 94, 97, 98, 102, 104, 108, 109, 112, 114, 115, 117, 119, 123, 125, 131, 133, 134, 135, 136, 137, 142, 143, 145, 146, 149, 153, 156, 158, 163, 164, 165, 173, 177, 178, 182, 187, 191, 194, 200, 202, 213, 217, 219, 232, 233, 235, 236, 238, 241, 244, 250, 251

Copyright K. Beaty/*Toronto Star*: 197